Finding
Hidden
Profits

A Guide for Custom Builders

Dennis Dixon

Home Builder Press®
National Association of Home Builders
1201 15th Street, NW
Washington, DC 20005-2800
(800) 223-2665
www.builderbooks.com

Finding Hidden Profits: A Guide for Custom Builders

ISBN 0-86718-451-5

© 1999 by the National Association of Home Builders of the United States

Cover by David Rhodes, Art Director, Home Builder Press

Printed in the United States of America

Library of Congress Cataloging in Publication Data

Dixon, Dennis, 1954-
    Finding hidden profits : a guide for custom builders / Dennis Dixon.
        p.   cm.
    Includes bibliographical references (p.   ).
    ISBN 0-86718-451-5
    1. Construction industry—United States. 2. Building trades—United States. 3. Residential real estate—United States. 4. Architect-designed houses—United States. 5. Real estate investment—United States. 6. Real estate developers—United States. I. Title.
HD9715.U52D59   1998
692'.5—dc21   98-45914
                                           CIP

For more information please contact: Home Builder Press®
National Association of Home Builders
1201 15th Street, NW
Washington, DC 20005-2800
(800) 223-2665
http://www.nahb.com/builderbooks

Additional copies of this publication are available from Home Builder Press. NAHB members receive a 20 percent member discount on publications purchased through Home Builder Press. Quantity discounts also are available.

12/98 Harlowe/Hutchison 1500
02/00 Reprint 1000

Table of Contents

"The harder I work, the luckier I get."
Bert Pitre

"Work smart, work hard, and know what you're worth."
Bruce Larsen

Preface

The success of my company is based on quality and craftsmanship. We complete as many tasks as possible with our own employees; subcontract work is always carried out with the same craftspeople. Our subcontractors work hand-in-hand with us to produce finely crafted, customized, quality products for our clients.

Initially, my company goal was based on the "cooperative quality" of the finished custom home—not money. Unfortunately, craftsmanship is not the only essential component of a custom home builder's success. Without profitability custom home builders cannot survive.

My experiences in the construction business forced me to figure out ways to insure profitability. Dixon Builders completed several custom home projects that turned out beautifully, the owner was pleased, the job came in on time, but the profit just was not there. I found out the hard way that the quality of business management must be at the same level as the craftsmanship of the finished product.

Profitability in construction is directly proportional to the contractor being organized, professional, and a capable manager. Anticipating problems and solving them ahead of time is one of the main experience factors used to differentiate among custom home builders.

In my experience as a longtime director of my local NAHB chapter and an advisor for members, I have learned that builders, suppliers, and subcontractors always can improve their business skills. I am always learning. I have found that making money is directly proportional to organization and proper administration of the business aspect of home building.

Acknowledgments

The author would like to thank some of the people that advised, guided, and helped him succeed as a builder: Michael and Katherine Jane Dixon, Bud Archer, Dick Bailey, Barney and Jeanne Dreyfuss, Jim Hoselton, Bert and Dody Pitre, Chuck Putnik, Hal Rich, Peter Rich, Bill Shaler, Ron Todd, and especially my wife Jan Pitre-Dixon.

Many thanks also to Terry Lawson for drawing the humorous side of the construction business.

The authors and Home Builder Press wish to acknowledge the contributions of the following reviewers who assisted with reviews of the proposal or the developing manuscript: Jim Carr, Ohio State University, Wooster, OH; Allan Freedman, National Association of Home Builders staff, Washington, D.C.; Jim Graves, Graves-Harshman and Co., Inc., Flagstaff, AZ; Stephen K. Hann, Stephen K. Hann Custom Builders, Houston, TX; Mark D. Kalin, Kalin Custom Homes, Inc., Smithville, MO; Ray Killian, Jr., Simonini Builders, Inc., Charlotte, NC; John Lane, Lane and Associates, Fort Smith, AK; Fred

Parker, Fort Worth, TX; E. Lee Reid, Riverview, FL; William Saint, Simonini Builders, Inc., Charlotte, NC; and Alan Simonini, Simonini Builders, Inc., Charlotte, NC.

Finding Hidden Profits: A Guide for Custom Builders was produced under the general direction of Kent Colton, NAHB Executive Vice President and CEO, in association with NAHB staff members James E Johnson, Jr. , Staff Vice President, Information Services Division; Adrienne Ash, Assistant Staff Vice President, Publishing Services; Charlotte McKamy, Publisher; Sharon Lamberton, Acquiring Editor; Kurt Lindblom, Project Manager; David Rhodes, Art Director; Barbara Minich, Copyeditor and Proofreader; and Thayer Long, Assistant Editor.

About
the Author

Dennis A. Dixon is a licensed general contractor for both residential and commercial projects. Since 1984, Dixon Builders has completed more than 60 custom homes, more than 40 custom remodels, and numerous commercial projects.

Dixon is currently a member of the board of directors of his local home builder association (Northern Arizona Home Builders), as well as one of its past presidents.

For several years Dixon hosted a radio program entitled Home Talk that dealt with all issues of construction and real estate. He is also a nationally recognized speaker addressing issues, problems, and solutions facing custom home builders and remodelers and other construction industry professionals. Subjects include "Finding Hidden Profits in Custom Home Construction (via Allowances, Change Orders, and Specifications)," "Low-Cost, Simple Detail Ideas that Improve Your Quality," and "Improving Your Profits, Cash Flow, and Income During an Economic Downturn."

Introduction

Profit is the money received by a company when it sells a product or service for more money than it costs to produce it.

For the purposes of this book, profit is the money a builder earns from a project after the hard costs for materials, labor, and administrative expenses are paid. With this money, the builder is able to maintain a cash flow, make investments, and develop new projects.

Profit is different than your salary. Your salary is an annual amount that your company pays you on a regular basis in exchange for your knowledge, expertise, and management abilities.

Profit is calculated as a percentage of your expenses. To maximize your profit, you must know all your expenses. Smart builders research each cost before they bid the job. On top of the obvious costs for time, materials, fees, permits, etc., they add their overhead costs, including their salary. For every expense that you estimate too low or forget to include, you lose profit.

Why? Because profit dollars are determined by markup. Markup represents the difference between the cost to the builder and the selling price to the owner. Markup is a percentage based on the project's cost. The more accurate your costs, the higher the total amount on which markup is calculated.

For example, the total costs for time and materials, fees, permits, etc., for a custom home is $450,000. With a 10 percent markup, the selling price of the home is $495,000, with a profit of $45,000. If you add in $50,000 for your overhead and salary, the cost of the custom home increases to $500,000. The selling price is $550,000 with a 10 percent markup and your profit increases to $50,000—with your overhead costs and salary paid. The $550,000 selling price more accurately reflects your costs and the profit due your company.

I have a favorite parable about profit and markup that I have updated with current characters and terms.

> A man is attending his high school's 20-year reunion. This man is a billionaire and runs a store chain with more than 100 stores. All the attendees are curious about the successful classmate who never did well in school and was horrible in math.
>
> After some coaxing by his classmates, the billionaire steps up to the podium and addresses the class about his success. He begins: "I know a lot of you are curious about my financial success. I never did well in school and still I'm not very good at math. But my success is due to one simple rule, I operate my business on a 1 percent markup. Whatever I buy for a dollar I sell for two!"

Well, the billionaire still isn't very good at math, but he sure knows how to make money. In truth, the successful classmate operates on a 100-percent markup because he doubles the price of everything he sells. Judging by his success, he has figured out how to include his overhead costs in the cost of the items to maximize his profit.

The percentage of profit is relative. When sales volumes are large, a business usually can operate on a smaller markup or percentage of profit. Contractors building custom homes, however, often have a limited amount of resources, labor, skilled help, and time. Usually, a limited number of high-end custom homes are built each year, so profits must be determined on a small number of projects, each of which has a high selling price.

Because your profits are dependent on a few projects, it is essential that you protect the profit you have in a job and look for additional profit centers.

Allowances and change orders both are potential profit centers for custom home builders. Accurately price the item to include time and materials, overhead costs, and your profit.

Retainers and consulting fees are another opportunity for custom home builders to make a profit. Do not give away your expertise, but look for opportunities to receive payment for your experience and knowledge.

A professional image based on quality and excellent management skills is yet another source for profits. Builders recognize that they must pick the client as carefully as the client selects a builder. A professional image results in more opportunities, which in turn allows the builder to be more selective and command a higher markup.

Finding Hidden Profits: A Guide for Custom Builders provides tips and suggestions that will enable you to both protect and increase your profits in seven areas:

- Determining overhead, salary, and profits

- Preparing accurate bids

- Calculating allowances

- Pricing change orders

- Customizing draw schedules

- Detailing builder specifications

- Writing comprehensive contracts

Many builders overlook the opportunities for making a profit from these custom home tools. Following the procedures outlined in the following chapters will help you profitably manage individual projects and achieve your business goals.

1

Calculate How Much Profit Is Enough

Contractor profit, for the purposes of this book, is defined as the amount of money remaining after all hard costs—overhead including salaries, subcontractors, suppliers, labor, and management fees—are paid. Do not confuse profit with office overhead, administrative costs, or your monthly salary.

Knowing your costs is fundamental to finding hidden profits in custom home construction. If you know your costs, you can reduce the amount of valuable time you spend with clients that cannot afford the product and services your company provides. You also can adequately price a project to protect your profit percentage.

Historically, statistics have shown that new businesses fail within the first year. This is due to a variety of reasons. The main cause, however, is an improper understanding of the amount of cash you must have on hand to operate and sustain a business during the first year. Operating a business without knowing precisely what your costs are is a formula for failure.

Builders bring a treasure chest of expertise, experience, knowledge, and managerial skills to a custom home project. Yet, even the most astute builder cannot succeed without making a profit.

Determine Your Costs

Determining the cash operating costs for a construction business is based on facts—actual expenses and actual invoices. The process is simple; there is no room for guessing. The formula is generated using the information listed below.

1. Determine the annual cost to run your office by adding up these expenses: rent, insurance, vehicle expense, office equipment, utilities, janitorial, telephone, etc.

2. Determine the annual costs for supervisory field employees: supervisor's salary, labor overhead, perks, vacation pay, etc.

3. Add in the annual salary for the officers (owners). Compensate officers realistically. Plug in $5,000 to $10,000 per month. What compensation do other professional make who gross $1 million per year?

4. Add in an amount for profit. Start at 10 percent of annual sales. Use your own target if it is more.

Summarize the cash costs for items 1 through 4. Divide that number by the number of weeks (52) in a year to get your out-of-pocket cash costs per week. This overhead and profit expense is the amount of money you need each week just to keep your doors open! And you haven't even built anything!

You can pinpoint your overhead expenses at a more tangible level by dividing the weekly cost by five days or by 40 working hours per week to determine your overhead costs per hour. Knowing your hourly, daily, and weekly expenses will be an incentive for you to control and manage your company. Time truly is money!

Let's consider an example. Your annual overhead expenses are listed below:

Office equipment	$ 300
Office insurance	1,300
Liability insurance	5,000
Office labor	45,000
Office miscellaneous	2,500
Office rent	15,600
Office supplies	1,500
Office telephone (all)	3,600
Office utilities	2,400
Office vehicles	12,800

Total $90,000

In our example it costs $90,000 in overhead costs to operate your office for one year. This calculates out to:

$90,000 per year/256 working days per year = $353 per day

$353 per day/8 working hours per day = $44 per hour

Add to the $90,000 overhead costs your salary and the total increases:

Office overhead .... $ 90,000
Owner compensation   120,000   ($10,000 per month)

Total $210,000

This new figure calculates out to:

$210,000 per year/256 working days per year = $820 per day

$820 per day/8 working hours per day = $102.50 per hour

Let's consider an example that illustrates how you can lose money doing simple tasks.

Every custom home builder has performed "favors" for clients and owners that are not compensated. Doing one or two favors a month, such as changing an outdoor, hard-to-reach light bulb, is good business practice. But what would happen if your employees started doing such favors 25 to 30 times a week?

What is a fair amount of compensation to change a light bulb if it takes 20 minutes to set the ladder and change the bulb?

One 60-watt bulb .... $ .90
1/3 hour labor @ $102.50/hour 34.00
Ladder use 5.00

Total $39.90

This sounds like an unreasonable cost for a simple task—and it still doesn't include the actual costs to bill and collect the charge. But this total—$39.90—is a cost based on facts.

To cover costs and ensure that such tasks do not cut into profits, many vendors and tradespeople have enacted a minimum charge, service fee, or trip charge of $50 to $100.

With this information, take the time to calculate your company's actual rough operating expenses. The numbers will astonish you. All of a sudden you're going to realize how much out-of-pocket cash (overhead) it costs your company to have your superintendent spend two hours walking a homeowner through the house. Or the amount of money it costs your company when you spend three hours researching and preparing change orders for items you don't think the owner truly wants. Knowing your overhead costs allows you to properly price, manage, and profit from bids, allowances, and change orders.

Allocate Your Overhead Costs

Once you have calculated what it costs to operate your company, other questions will pop up about how you allocate the costs:

- Should the overhead costs be divided among projects?
- Should I assign each job an overhead amount?
- Do I prorate overhead costs based on each project's contract amount?
- Should the costs be prorated based on job complexity, anticipated effort, hands-on management requirements?
- Do my office overhead costs vary? If so, by how much?

The general answer to the overhead/profit job-cost-assignment question is best explained with an example.

Smith Builders constructs four custom home projects in a given year. The company's gross sales dollars average about $1,200,000 per year.

Annual overhead costs	$ 90,000
Annual owner salary	120,000
Annual anticipated profit (10%)	120,000
Total annual overhead and profit costs . . .	**$330,000**

Smith Builders needs to generate $330,000 for overhead and profit from four jobs they will undertake and complete during the calendar year.

Smith Builders can assign its overhead/profit burdens two ways:

1. An equal amount of overhead/profit can be assigned to each job. If $330,000 is divided by 4, the amount each project must generate is $82,500. This method is simple as long as the jobs are similar in work, effort, time to complete, and gross dollar amounts.

$330,000/four projects × 100% = 25%

$330,000 × 25% = $82,500

2. The overhead/profit can be prorated based on the actual value of the construction contracts as a percentage of annual sales. The overhead burden is distributed among the jobs proportionally in this example.

$330,000/$1,200,000 × 100 = 27.5%

Job 1 Contract amount	$300,000 × 27.5%	=	$ 82,500
Job 2 Contract amount	$279,800 × 27.5%	=	$ 76,945
Job 3 Contract amount	$454,000 × 27.5%	=	$124,850
Job 4 Contract amount	$166,200 × 27.5%	=	$ 45,705
Totals $1,200,000			$330,000

To take this another step, let's use Job 1 as an example and look at the cost estimate, bid amount, and final contract process.

Job 1 Contract amount $300,000
Smith Builders' overhead/profit . . . . (82,500)

Production cash cost (expenses) $217,500

Smith Builders total cash outlay for subcontractors, suppliers, materials, freight, cleanup, errors, permits, sales taxes, etc., must not exceed $217,500 or the company will not meet its profit projections for the year and for that individual job. Every dollar that is spent over and above the $217,500 production cost is money directly out of the contractor's pocket.

The cost calculation and line-by-line estimate for Job 1 must not exceed $217,500 or the job is underbid.

If the cost estimation is prepared first, a proven method for success, then the overhead/profit burden can be adjusted accordingly. The final bid amount presented to the client is realistic and based on research, experience, and homework—not an off-the-cuff cost quote.

Prepare Accurate Estimates

Preparing an accurate cost estimate is part of being a professional custom home builder. Anyone who considers using square footage or "ballparking" to estimate costs for a custom home is practicing poor management skills. A good estimate requires a minimum of 100 cost-category line items or more. The more detail, the more accurate your estimate will be.

If you cannot do a proper estimate due to time constraints, poor plan quality, too many open-ended issues—for whatever reason—then pass on the job. There is a profitable difference between guessing and estimating!

Chapter 3, Prepare Accurate Bids, discusses in detail bid preparation and the importance of accurate estimates.

Decide How Much to Charge

As a custom home builder, you have to know what your services are worth and therefore, what to charge. Quality driven, professional custom home builders are few and far between. They service a segment of the market that is concerned more with the appearance of the finished product than with the cost to produce that product.

Numerous market factors influence what a builder can charge. In addition, banks, mortgage lenders, title companies, and other institutions that oversee the project have opinions about a "reasonable" profit for the job.

Banks and mortgage lenders require builders to submit a document that is unique to the building industry—the cost breakdown. Builders must list costs category-by-category. The banks use this information for a variety of reasons, one of which is to monitor where the money is going.

At the end of the cost breakdown, banks want to see a "reasonable" profit figure. Most institutions accept a line item for contractor profit as part of the budget process. To be acceptable, however, the percentage for that line item generally must be between 5 and 15 percent. Can you recoup your overhead and profit costs with 15 percent? In the example above, the percentage applied to the four jobs was 27.5 percent.

Present Actual Costs

Negotiating over the amount of money that a project will cost is common business practice. Defining and producing a custom home that fits the owner's needs, caliber of quality, and budget is part of the professional services you offer. Arguing over expenses and compensation to you, your company, and your subcontractors, however, is futile.

To reduce any questions, document your costs. Prepare paperwork that lists your actual overhead costs, subcontractor bids, and supplier quotes. Part of the professional function of a custom home builder is taking care of the support paperwork and documentation that goes along with a project.

It is no one's business but yours what your overhead, salary, and profit margins are. You and you alone are responsible for bringing to fruition the finished custom home and for the operation of your business. You determine your compensation. You determine your profits.

As you prepare the cost breakdown and list the line-by-line items, remember that is it perfectly acceptable to provide category line items for overhead expenses such as contingency, equipment, insurance, site security, supervision, utilities, and temporary services, etc. Document these costs and include them in your cost breakdown.

Consider the financial example below.

Smith Builders
Project Costs for Ryan Residence

Overhead costs (annual):

Administrative (office) labor costs	$ 70,100
Marketing/public relations	10,000
Insurance	8,500
Miscellaneous	2,500
Office equipment	3,000
Office janitorial	2,400
Office rent	12,000
Office supplies	4,000
Office utilities	3,600
Owner salary	120,000
Owner benefits	7,500
Postage	600
Corporate taxes	(not included)
Telephone	10,000
Tool/equipment expense	12,300
Vehicle expense	21,500
Worker's compensation insurance	12,000
Total annual overhead costs	**$300,000**

Summary:

Total annual overhead costs	$ 300,000
Combined hard costs for Ryan home	$1,650,000
Selling price of Ryan home	$2,000,000
Profit after expenses are paid	**$ 50,000**

In this example, the $50,000 profit is 2.5 percent of the selling price of the home.

$50,000/$2,000,000 × 100 = 2.50%

The owner is receiving a monthly salary, which is included in the overhead costs. As it should be, the salary is part of the business's operating expenses. The full compensation for the owner in the above example is $170,000 ($120,000 salary + $50,000 profit).

A second example uses the same selling price for the home and hard costs, but the owner's salary is include in the profit and not the overhead.

Summary:
Total annual overhead costs . . . .$ 180,000
Combined hard costs for Ryan home   . . .$1,650,000
Selling price of Ryan home $2,000,000
Profit after expenses are paid . . . .$ 170,000

$170,000 = $50,000 profit + $120,000 owner's salary

In this example, the profit is 8.5 percent of the home's selling price.

$170,000/$2,000,000 \times 100 = 8.50\%$

To take the example one step further, do not include overhead costs in the expenses, but add them into the profit. The costs follow.

Summary:
Combined hard costs for Ryan home   . . .$1,650,000
Selling price of Ryan home $2,000,000
Profit after expenses are paid . . . .$ 350,000

$350,000 = $50,000 profit + $300,000 overhead costs

In this example, the profit line is 17.5 percent.

$350,000/$2,000,000 \times 100 = 17.50\%$

In all three examples, you have the same hard costs and the same selling price. The overhead costs, owner's salary, and "profit" also are the same. The difference is how they are presented to the bank and owner on the cost breakdown. Keeping in mind that most banks are comfortable with a profit of 5 to 15 percent, which way would you present the information? Is it worth taking a chance that the bank will not fund the third example because the 17.5 percent is considered too high?

CASE STUDY #1.1

Watch Those Percentages!

Smith Builders owner Bill Smith has a three-year history of grossing more than $1 million per year. His take-home profit, however, is hard to pinpoint due to poor accounting methods, jobs that cross calendar years, etc.

Bill Smith has identified the following business goals:

1. Make $125,000 next year ($60,000 salary + $65,000 profit).
2. Cover office overhead operating costs of $28,000.
3. Build 3 houses during the year.

Bill Smith needs to generate $51,000 per custom home to cover his salary of $125,000 and pay for his overhead expenses.

$125,000 + $28,000 = $153,000/3 homes = $51,000

How can Bill Smith accomplish his business goals?

Smith Builders is bidding Project #1, a 3,000-square-foot home with a 910-square-foot three-car garage. The costs are listed below.

Construction hard-costs estimate $251,668
Office overhead cost ($28,000/3 projects) . . . $ 9,333
Project #1 Cash Cost $261,001
Smith Builders profit requirement . . . . $ 51,000
Project #1 bid price $312,001

Project facts

1. The project is being bid at $104 per square foot of living space ($312,001/3,000 sq. ft. = $104).

2. Bill Smith's salary of $5,000 per month is part of the $51,000 included in the sales price. The home will take six months to complete so Bill Smith's salary will equal $30,000 or 59 percent of the $51,000 (30,000/ $51,000 × 100 = 59.0%).

3. The $21,000 leftover after Bill Smith's salary is subtracted is the percentage of job profit—the icing on the cake.

With these figures and facts, which is the best way to present the information to the bank and owner? You decide which formula fits your needs in your market.

Option A: Profit/Sales Price = Percent Profit
$51,000/$312,001 × 100 = 16.34% profit

Option B: Profit—Salary/Contract Amount × 100 = Percent Profit
$51,000 – $30,000 = $21,000/$312,001 × 100 = 6.73% profit

Case Study #1.1 provides another example of how allocating costs can change the profit percentage.

Maintain Your Profits to Maintain Your Salary

Most small business owners fall victim to financial circumstances that demand they reinvest their own capital in their business to keep it afloat. For a variety of reasons, there aren't any cash reserves on hand to carry the business through a bad business cycle or slow cash-flow period.

Avoiding this condition is simple. Maintain your profitability and the ability of your business to pay your salary. The financial pressures you feel are a constant reminder of the daily battle to keep your company on track, profitable, and directed properly.

The inability to pay yourself due to poor cash flow, slow client payments, or poor planning is an indication of a bigger problem. Profitability enables your company to weather the slow times. If you are not making a profit, you're doing something wrong. If the profit goes, so will your salary.

As the driving force behind the creation of a unique art form known as the custom home, you deserve professional compensation. Set your own standards. Adjust your expenses and costs as to what the market will endure, get the job done, and make a profit.

Make sure your goals, morals, and standards are understood and shared by the client. Align yourself and your company with clients that perceive your professionalism.

2

Take Charge of the Project

On a custom home jobsite only one person is in charge: you! As the builder, you are responsible for constructing the custom home. Therefore you, and only you, sit behind the Harry S. Truman desk bearing the placard "The buck stops here."

As the "Captain of the Ship," you have control over the profitability of the project. You sign the contract, oversee the bid and budget process, hire subcontractors and suppliers, and correct everyone else's mistakes. You assume all duties associated with creating a finely crafted, well constructed, durable, everlasting custom residence that satisfies the owners and earns a profit for your company.

Any project you undertake should be with the understanding that you alone will run and manage the jobsite. Clients hire you to take responsibility for the project and to exercise the authority that comes with it. Responsibility and authority go hand-in-hand. Being the leader requires an active, not passive role.

Enhance your reputation among team members by assuming the authority that is yours as the builder. If you

You are captain of the ship. Assume the authority with the responsibility and guide the project along a path to profitability.

exercise care and show a personal interest in quality, so will those who work on the project with you. Build a team that will complete the project on time and at the highest quality level and you will find new opportunities for profit. Subcontractors will want to work with you, suppliers will look forward to your business, and new clients will call your office because they recognize your professionalism. Pick your clients with care and assert your right to earn a profit.

Learn to Delegate

While you are in charge of the project, given the scope of your responsibilities you must be able to delegate authority. Most successful builders undertake more than one project at a time. To do this effectively, they delegate authority through a job foreperson or superintendent.

Delegation of authority is a skill that every good businessperson learns to do if they are going to manage multiple operations successfully. The superintendent acts as the coordinator, quality control person, and facilitator on the job every minute of every production day. He or she oversees the details, but the contractor provides the direction.

"I took shop in high school, can I help?"

A custom project requires hands-on management and a physical presence at the jobsite to coordinate the work as it progresses and enforce the jobsite rules. Providing direction and supervision is more practical than missing details and tearing out work to correct it.

It is up to you to delegate authority. Find someone you trust who will follow your rules and keep you informed. Remember, however that your name is on the license, bond, and insurance.

Communicate Successfully

Communication between you and the owner is essential to the successful production and completion of a custom home project. Without constant, positive, and meaningful interaction, the job will have problems.

Successful builders also recognize the need to build and maintain communications with all the parties involved with the project—architect, appraiser, banker, inspector, and tradespeople.

Be specific with subcontractors and suppliers. Put your requirements in writing so everyone understands what is needed. Request bids in writing so you understand the cost and what will be provided.

Even one of our country's founding fathers and past presidents had trouble with communications during one phase of the constant remodeling that was occurring at Monticello over a 40-year period.

> As the story goes, Jefferson brought some skilled European tradesmen from another area to complete the oak, cherry, and birch parquet flooring of the parlor. Jefferson outlined what he wanted and the tradesmen provided a verbal estimate. When the floor was completed, Jefferson was ecstatic with the look and the quality, but was flabbergasted at the finished price—the equivalent of $200. He eventually paid the carpenters, but some was in cash, some in barter, and some in foodstuffs.
>
> History has repeated this story of misunderstanding in nearly every custom home project since! (*Jefferson's Monticello*, by William Howard Adams, Abbeville Press, New York, NY; 1985.)

Effective communications contribute to the project's profit opportunities. Use communications skills to reach the following goals:

1. Satisfy the owner.

2. Build a professional reputation with all other parties.

3. Understand and identify the team players and coordinate their roles to the advantage of the project.

4. Maximize quality by exercising personal attention to the project to achieve higher profitability.

Make Communications Personable

Communication should always be personable. One-on-one interaction is best. Make primary contact either in person or by telephone and then follow-up by putting pertinent details in writing.

Keeping subcontractors and suppliers up-to-date with changes and job conditions promotes professionalism. Quality is maintained. Safety is improved. Liability risk is reduced. As a result, insurance premiums remain low and steady, which in turn enhances profitability. Case Study #2.1

CASE STUDY #2.1

What Warning Is Sufficient?

Custom homes tend to draw curious visitors that want to walk through the project. Turning the jobsite into a fenced fort is one way to maintain safety and keep visitors away. Another is to use proper signage—Stop: No Entry Construction Personnel Only; Warning: Open Trench; No Trespassing; Danger—Construction Zone; Open Pit—No Admittance.

Consider this story. A construction site was closed down for the weekend. Signs and flagging were posted to keep out visitors. But a neighbor walking his dog entered the premises. The dog was on a leash and somehow slipped into an open footing trench and impaled itself on a #4 vertical rebar. The owner of the dog brought suit against the contractor for negligence and was awarded some funds from the insurance carrier out of court.

Resolution: Ask your insurance carrier what signage and protections are recommended. Have the same discussion with your attorney. I recommend always posting signage on all sides of the jobsite. And always use rebar caps.

illustrates how communications through signage can help reduce your liability risk.

As the general contractor, you are the only person who can set the tone and the overall attitude surrounding a custom home project. A positive outlook, compliments on the workmanship of others, and cushioned criticism go a long way toward maintaining an even course toward project completion.

Your crew will follow your positive, productive directions. You need team effort to maintain quality and meet the completion date. Keep everything in perspective and manage the things that you have control over. If necessary, take someone aside and work out a problem. This is always the best solution.

Communicate with Owners

My experience has exposed me to many different types of owners and their personalities. All owners want to be involved with their custom home. By definition, that's part of the process.

Keep communications personable. One-on-one is best. Make primary contact either in person or by telephone and then follow up by putting pertinent details in writing.

Weekly or biweekly progress reports impress owners and keep surprises to a minimum. The reports personalize the project and your hands-on management skills.

How can an owner be out of touch with the project when progress reports are consistent, informative, and timely?

Summarize the schedule, weather problems, progress, or lack thereof. This eliminates the possibility that the owner will delay final payment because of a problem that goes back to the first month of the job.

The progress report also helps resolve problems in a timely manner. Attorneys will confirm that any future legal problems are solved more easily when routine communications are provided to the owner. An owner cannot claim that he or she was kept in the dark when there are 25 progress reports that documented the project as it progressed. Make sure the reports document both the good and not so good. An owner will never fault you for keeping them informed. Delaying or avoiding bad news never helps. Waiting and hoping for a miracle is foolhardy. Figure 2.1 is an example of a progress report.

You also can use past experience to personalize custom homes for the individual owners with a "hot button list" that indicates your knowledge and willingness to accommodate their needs. The hot button list is included in Figure 2.2.

Identify the Primary Players

Identify the owner's representative and the contractor's representative in the contract. In each case, designate only one person. Note that all communications take place with these individuals.

The owner's representative signs allowances, change orders, clarification change orders, draw requests, and any other relevant documents. This makes the owner's representative the ultimate decision maker at the "home office" and eliminates confusion about which owner signs, approves, or initiates decisions on the project.

The owner's representative—and no one else—coordinates influence, suggestions, and comments from architects, bankers, appraisers, and friends. This keeps the owner's "helpers" at arms length from the contractor's representative and avoids miscommunications.

As the contractor, you are the contractor's representative. You have the authority to make adjustments, alterations, interpretations, and change orders. The chain of command dictates that your employees and subcontractors accept direction only from you.

You sign all paperwork. For example, you are the only person authorized to approve, price, change costs, and waive fees associated with change orders. This procedure shields the job superintendent from requests for information.

FIGURE 2.1 Progress Report #13

Date: October 18, 1999—Week 26

Project: Thomason Residence
               Lot 593 Forest Meadows Estates
               5137 North Windy Walk Way
               Flagstaff, Arizona 86001

Contractor: Smith Custom Builders (Bill Smith)
               Flagstaff, Arizona
               (520) 555-1212

1. Framing is complete. Several small carpentry tasks remain, such as blocking, hurricane strapping, etc. Inspection is scheduled for Tuesday next week.

2. Roofing tiles have been delivered. Several of the pallets (6 out of 18 total) were damaged and must be replaced. Waiting for the new material will delay completing the roof by about 2 weeks.

3. The architect will have the final detailing to us by Nov. 1 on the skylight changes. Alterations will be completed prior to the roofing.

4. Plumbing top out begins today. Electrical rough-in will start mid next week.

5. Submittal drawings for the iron railings were completed Tuesday, October 13, 1999. Aspen Steel Fabricators will have the exterior and interior railings completed ahead of schedule.

6. Change orders 27 through 32 are enclosed. Please review, sign, and return payment to my office as soon as you can (before Friday, October 25, 1999). Thanks.

7. The bank inspector requested insurance verification from the plastering contractor. That information has been provided to the bank.

8. The driveway access will have an open trench in it next week for the gas line. Be careful when you enter the jobsite.

9. House completion will be in 16 weeks (February 20, 2000).

10. Mr. Johnson (neighbor) stopped by yesterday and complimented us on keeping the street clean and free of construction debris. I have stopped by to see him several times in recent weeks to make sure our work is not a problem for him.

If you have any questions or comments on this information, please feel free to contact me.

Bill Smith

FIGURE 2.2 Owner Hot Button Detailing List

1. At what height should shower heads be placed? Depending on the height of the owner, you might want to go higher than 6 feet, 6 inches.

2. What countertop height is comfortable for the master bath vanity?
   - How deep should the master bath medicine cabinet be—4 inches or 12 inches?
   - Can you make the master bath vanity tops 36 inches deep?
   - Will beveled bath mirrors give a more custom look?

3. If the countertop height for the master bath vanity is adjusted, should the kitchen countertops also be raised?

4. Are the owners left- or right-handed?
   - Which side of the kitchen sink is more convenient for the disposal switch?
   - On which side of the sink should the dishwasher be placed?
   - Is the trash pullout tray located adjacent to the disposal? Plan on using a full door height for the trash pullout. Use a width dimension so that a compactor can always be inserted as an option. The electrical connection is the disposal plug under the kitchen sink cabinet.

5. Are the door swings on the plan convenient or backwards according to intended room use and access?

6. Review the detailing of the garage, patio, pantry, hallway, laundry room, and special rooms, paying attention to the location of switches, plugs, phone jacks, etc. Even though our society uses all types of cordless phones, plan on installing 10 extra phone jacks.

7. Are plugs located in atypical spots for use in connecting a vacuum in hallways, closets, bedrooms, etc.? Plugs often are buried behind obvious places for furniture. Put in a few extra plugs for easy access.

8. Review locations for bath hardware before completing the framing. Blocking installed at the identified locations will assure that the bath hardware is installed well and won't continually come loose in the drywall.

9. Floor drains in the garage minimize winter snow muck that falls off the vehicles. Slope the floor in four directions towards the drain. Melting ice and snow then stay out of the people paths in the garage.

10. Review the owner's needs with regard to garage door openers. Install a keypad at the exterior doorjamb. Furnish a small key chain-type opener for owners to give to kids, friends, etc. One owner used his key chain opener as his "key" when he went bike riding.

11. Identify high traffic or vulnerable areas of the home where the carpet will wear quickly and order additional carpet for that area. The cost is minimal for enough extra carpeting to redo a 6-x-10-foot hallway when the owner's kids grow older. Replacing it is simple.

12. The framing stage always seems to generate scrap 2x and sheathing (plywood). Use that scrap to act as runners in the attic or platforms for additional storage space. Do it and then tell the owner what you provided.

FIGURE 2.2 *Continued*

13. Insulate everything. It makes energy sense and it's a minimal cost. If the local codes require R-30, use R-36. Exceed the minimum requirements for floors, interior walls, bathtubs, etc. If there is a void space, fill it. The house will sound more solid, rooms will stay either warmer or cooler and sound transmission will be minimized. This is the standard of a true custom home builder.

14. Review the job and come up with a list of five small details that you can do to improve the quality and customization of the home.
    - Can you do an extra shelf in the pantry?
    - Is there room to install both high and low clothes rods in the entry closet?
    - Use 3.5-inch screws to secure lock strikes at exterior doors.
    - Calk the baseboards and casing to the walls. Fill the small voids.
    - Use three hinges on doors, instead of two.

15. When the house is complete:
    - Leave several new light bulbs for fixtures (all types of bulbs used in the house).
    - Furnish the owner with a three-ring notebook with all of the owner's manuals, warranty cards, and paperwork.
    - Include an alphabetized cover sheet with the names and phone numbers of all pertinent subcontractors and suppliers. Also include information such as parcel number, property tax codes, permit number, lot number, etc.
    - Use your construction locks during construction. Keep the keys to the finished lock in your hands, not accessible to 10 people. Explain your policy to keep the finished home security intact.
    - Supply the keys to the owners at the final walk through. Give them five keys, not two.

16. Keep an eye on the detailing as it progresses. Fixing something later, instead of now, is a bad habit. Keep in mind your goal of 100-percent quality. Sometimes you have to settle for 90 percent, but is 75 percent acceptable in a home built by true craftspeople?

17. Use your knowledge and understanding of the owners and be sensitive to their interests, needs, quirks, desires, and wishes. It will reap rewards every time.

Jobsite personnel have any easy out because they can respond to the owner or the architect with four simple words: "Talk to the contractor."

Field personnel know they do not implement any changes without written approval from you. The owner can visit with the superintendent, but ultimately you must address all adjustments, questions, and what-ifs.

Likewise, you are responsible for discussing theoretical issues with the other professionals involved with the project, such as your job superintendent. Your direction and input enables them to concentrate on jobsite issues that keep the project moving forward.

Establish Jobsite Rules

Making money building custom homes is directly related to how well you and your subcontractors and suppliers interact on each project. As the builder, you set the standard and tone for the job. You are the leader, manager, pacesetter, and quality control inspector all rolled into one.

A set of jobsite rules and quality standards tells your subcontractors and suppliers in advance your expectations regarding the project. When you find subs and suppliers that share your goals and expectations, develop long-term relationships with them. Because custom home building is quality driven, not dollar driven, the relationships you foster will enable everyone involved in the project to make money.

This sounds like a simple, logical concept. In reality, however, it is more difficult to carry out. Without a set of rules, subcontractors and suppliers can make your life miserable. Having experienced this myself, I developed the following set of rules that I enforce at each jobsite.

Subcontractors and suppliers do not discuss business with clients. The subcontractor or supplier is on the project because I hired them. They are not on site to solicit additional business, initiate change orders, or complicate the structured process. I tell all my subcontractors and suppliers that they just have to remember four little words: "Talk to the contractor."

Pricing is only quoted at retail. I am the only person to quote a price and my policy is to quote retail.

Contractor discounts are never discussed, reviewed, or acknowledged. I reward the loyalty of my subcontractors and suppliers with continued business, quick and timely payments, and removal of problems caused by outside interference. In return I receive discounts that figure in my profit.

Allowing an owner to negotiate prices with a supplier is not part of my process. If any negotiating with an owner is to be done, I do it. Using the same subcontractors and suppliers repeatedly makes my business life easier because all parties know what to expect. Every custom home is business as usual and the training and explaining ritual is minimized.

The jobsite is a place for work and craftsmanship, not a picnic ground. No smoking, no drinking (even after hours), and no loud radios are allowed at my jobsites. If you have to explain the list of nos more than once to any subcontractor or supplier, it's time to find a new one!

Outline the Allowance Process

Outline in advance the process by which the owner is to select allowance items. My construction contract lists the approved subcontractors and suppliers for each project. I provide the job specifications to the supplier ahead of time. I take these steps so that I can control the allowance selection process.

I am involved with the setup of appointments at suppliers' showrooms for the owner selection process. Some contractors even are present during this process to avoid miscommunications or ill provided direction.

Make sure the owner speaks to a trusted, experienced salesperson. Ask the salesperson to limit choices by price, cost, color, or decorator theme constraints. Request that he or she pull out three grades of carpet selections ahead of time that are within the owner's budget. If the owner then wanders around and decides on a custom-colored, imported wool carpet, the owner made the decision to step outside the realm of the given choices and allowance constraints.

For pricing, my suppliers have two options: quote only retail prices or tell the owner that I, as the contractor, will quote the prices.

To the owner, I emphasize that the items listed as allowances are to be supplied by a company with which I do business. An unknown supplier or installer can wreak havoc on the project's progress and your bottom line. Naming the approved personnel and companies ahead of time eliminates the ever-present owner concept: "Well my son works for ABC Drywall Company and they're out of work, can they drywall my house?"

Organize and Manage Tasks

A profitable contractor is synonymous with a good manager. Visiting the job-site and evaluating progress, providing direction, and solving big-picture problems are all management tasks. A custom home contractor wearing a tool belt is not doing his or her job. The contractor needs to manage—cash flow, paperwork, progress, closing the next project—all the while monitoring the quality of the work at hand.

Good management and organization is the only genuine pathway to profitability. Paperwork and business details are traditionally not the enjoyable aspect of home building. These jobs are not perceived as profitable. But that is wrong!

In the 80s and 90s, the perception of a builder in overalls driving a beat-up pickup truck was replaced with a more professional image. Today, many builders are college educated and have sales, marketing, and management skills that match the complexity of the custom homes they build.

Keeping with the professional image, I have four business skills that I believe builders must follow to be profitable.

Set up a business office with basic business equipment. Establish an office where official business is conducted, records are filed, and people can reach you.

Create an operations plan. Generate a mission statement that answers the question: What is your company all about? Outline the tasks and responsibilities that are your responsibility and those that are delegated to others. Describe what is expected of each employee, who supervises onsite work, and who coordinates the project's scheduling, ordering, and paperwork.

Establish procedures for how paperwork will be generated, organized, and completed. Save and file everything. Date the paper, note where it came from, and who authorized it. Every job should have 10 to 20 files depending on the scope of work. You might be surprised at how good record keeping can save you money and provide a record as to which subcontractors and suppliers are doing adequate or poor paperwork.

Analyze your strengths and weaknesses. Make a list of things that you do well. Make another list of things you do poorly and consider delegating those tasks. As the contractor, you set the level of quality and the standards for employees, subcontractors, and suppliers. Set realistic goals for yourself, your employees, and your subcontractors. Set the quality standard by paying attention to details. Take the time to get organized and learn management skills. As your abilities increase, so will your profits.

3

Prepare Accurate Bids

Bidding on a custom home project is like walking through a minefield. Before you submit a quote, do your homework thoroughly or the job might end up full of craters.

Always evaluate the job, the client, and the circumstances before you enter into a bid agreement. As a custom home builder you will be asked to spend more productive hours bidding custom work than any other professionals associated with the project. Whether you give away your time or earn a profit is up to you.

Profitability on any project is based on the accuracy of the cost estimate and the bid. If you can't do the homework, don't pursue the project.

Evaluate the Owner

Some owners who seek a bid from a custom builder are in reality trying to pick your brain. Responding to their requests is an opportunity for you to provide unpaid work, advice, and expertise.

I suspect this lack of compensation for submitting bids goes back to the maintenance handyman quoting "free estimates" for home repairs. Regardless

CASE STUDY #3.1

Do You Want to Work with this Client for 12 Months?

A contractor met with some potential owners who wanted to invest approximately $750,000 on a custom home. Both parties were interviewing one another during the course of the discussion.

The initial meeting went well and the builder started doing some estimating and scheduling for the project while the plans were being finalized.

Several circumstances started to unfold. The plans were of mediocre quality and consistency. The builder contacted the architect and he agreed with the quality of the plans. The owners had revised, revised, and re-revised the plans until the architect was fed up.

At the second business meeting, one of the owners inquired about being onsite to review the work as it progressed. It became apparent that the spouse wanted to be onsite daily and really run the job.

Resolution: The builder backed away from this "bad opportunity." Two strikes and you're out. Inconsistent plans and an owner who wants to play contractor are not good starting points.

of where it came from, it is an unpleasant aspect of the custom home building business.

Profitable custom home builders are able to distinguish opportunities for legitimate business from requests for free advice. Case Study #3.1 demonstrates a situation when it is best to walk away.

Evaluate the Project

Evaluate whether or not you want the job. Does it fit the talents of your company? Will it fit in with your current or upcoming jobs?

One of the best methods for minimizing wasted time is to spend some time interviewing the client and analyzing the circumstances. I use five criteria in my evaluation. If my response is positive for all five criteria I proceed cautiously with the project. If any of the five items are negative, I pass on the project.

The five project criteria I use are:

1. Is the budget realistic?

2. Are the plans and specifications of high quality?

3. Is the timetable realistic?

4. Are the client's expectations about the contractor reasonable?

5. Can I prepare a quality bid and cost estimate in a timely manner?

Be realistic, honest, and carefully evaluate the project information. Consider the long-term relationship. If you get a bad feeling from someone associated with the project, it is probably best to back away in a business-like manner: "Your project looks quite interesting, but at this point in time I cannot commit my company to another 10-month job."

Remember, working on a bad job will prevent you from taking on another good job. Bad jobs also tend to take more of your effort and patience, and they always have low profit centers.

Bid quality and accuracy is a requirement for any profitable job. A contractor who bids work by "guessing" costs is headed for disaster. If you cannot do a good job on the bid/cost estimate, you have no business bidding the job.

"My nephew, the Architecture student, says $138 a foot is too much money!"

Be realistic, honest, and careful when you evaluate the information from each project. Consider the long-term relationship. If you get a bad feeling from someone associated with the project, it is probably best to back away in a business-like manner.

Finally, if you cannot do an excellent job reviewing the plan and specifications, budgeting to determine costs, and compiling a list of possible cost estimating errors, don't bid the job. Do not bid the project unless you can do an A+ job on everything! You have nothing to gain and everything to lose. As a professional, you must know when you are outgunned and the forces of the marketplace are working against you.

4

Make Allowances a Profit Center

Just as you make money on every assembly piece, labor cost, and management effort, calculate a profit on allowances. Carefully determine the cost of every allowance item you touch, handle, oversee, or manage, and then add your profit.

The time you spend researching the costs and defining the parameters of each allowance improves your company's bottom line and the overall efficiency of your construction operation. Do not tolerate allowances as a necessary evil, but as an opportunity: "What profit can I make on door hardware...."

Allowances historically have not been a profit center for builders. You can earn profits with allowances and in the process minimize confusion. Make allowances profit opportunities, not money pits.

Use Calculated Allowances

Allowances are holes in the plans and specifications. Smart custom home builders to their best to plug these holes with calculated allowances. A calculated allowance is a "good faith effort" by the builder to provide the owner with a basis or starting point for an unselected item.

As a builder, you must solicit feedback from the owner or decorator regarding the budget and quality of product the owner desires. Combine this knowledge with your feel for the overall scope of the project and select a product in a specific cost and quality range that you think will satisfy the owner.

Then develop a calculated allowance that spells out and lists in detail the specific products, miscellaneous fees, and labor costs. Profitable builders add to this total their overhead costs and profit. After all, if you know the price of the carpet when you do your bid, you add your overhead and profit to the cost—why not do it with allowances?

Use the retail price to calculate the allowance and add your profit. The discount you negotiate with the subcontractor or supplier is payment for the volume of business you do, as well as your loyalty and fast-pay procedures.

> **Example:** A typical allowance category is door hardware. The owners are not sure what they want, but they like levers. The overall theme of the home is "rustic elegance" and much of the trim is detailed and done with knotty pine. Given this basic information, the builder selects a good quality lockset, in a finish that compliments the theme. To determine the allowance, the builder adds up all the doors, multiplies that number times the retail cost per lockset, adds the profit percentage, and assigns the allowance.

Answer these questions as you calculate the value of an allowance:

- How is the allowance amount defined?

- Are overhead costs, freight, handling, and installation included?

- What is the definition of the labor rate and how will it be determined?

- What is your profit and is it included in the allowance amount? Will your profit be charged as a percentage of the allowance spent?

- Are products selected as part of an allowance included in the overall warranty? How can a builder, subcontractor, or supplier warrant a product before that product is selected or defined?

- Are trade discounts passed along to the owner?

- If the owner's selections result in costs that exceed the allowance amounts by 50 percent or 200 percent, is the builder or architect guilty of misleading the owner?

An owner will always pose the key question about an allowance: "Is that enough? Can we get the stuff we want with that amount?" The only way to assure the owner and protect yourself is to clearly show the calculations and parameters you use to determine the allowance.

When you do a good job calculating allowance amounts, you're truly solving problems ahead of time. If the owner follows the normal path of the recommended allowance, your work level does not increase because it is part of the your "normal" routine. Products and services come from known subcontractors and suppliers, so there is not an ambiguity factor dealing with new people (who may or may not have your interest at heart). Should conflicts arise, resolve them with the owner as they occur.

Define Allowance Parameters

To keep these undefined and unanswered questions from becoming problems later, define each allowance as though it was a specification. Spell out the details, facts, and considerations, including what you do and do not recommend. Include what will and will not be covered under warranty, past experience with the performance and durability of certain products, etc.

"How was I to know that a $1,000 allowance for carpet wasn't enough? Now I'm supposed to cough up $5,500."

My experience shows that defining the details of an allowance category sometimes gently encourages the owner to make a decision right then and there: "Ah, let's just go with what the builder recommends and has had good experience with."

Explain Allowances in the Contract

In the contract, write out how you came up with the allowance amount. Spell out the calculated allowance in the appropriate category in the specifications. Use words and calculations that make it easy for owners and others to understand how the amount was determined.

Include language that spells out how you will handle allowances. Include the definition, dollar amount, and your terms and conditions regarding the allowance. Keep in mind the following points when you ask your attorney to draw up your contract.

Deadlines. Note the deadline selection date for each allowance. State that if the owner fails to complete their selections by the specified dates, the project may be delayed. Summarize allowance items and due dates on a single page in the contract to make it easy for the owner to locate and keep track of the requirements. Figure 4-1 is an example of an allowance summary sheet.

Reconciliation procedures. Summarize all allowance amounts in the construction contract. State that allowances will be defined, reconciled, and balanced with a written change order.

"I don't care if the contract says approved suppliers, I want you to buy my appliances at Discount City!"

Calculations. Define the allowances and the calculation methods, footnotes, etc., in the appropriate specification category.

Administrative fee. Allowance changes, adjustments, and alterations take time and effort. Make sure your company is compensated. Include an administrative fee that covers your time and effort: Allowances will be billed at the rate of $45 per hour (or whatever rate is acceptable to the builder). Use your office overhead costs as a guide. See Chapter 1, Calculate How Much Profit Is Enough, for examples.

Item sources. Note approved suppliers and subcontractors for allowance selections. State that only these companies may provide allowance items. Do not permit owners to supply or furnish allowance items. State that all products are purchased and provided by the general contractor through specified, approved vendors.

Time requirements. Make sure the allowance change order notes the time required to order and install the special order "custom" items. Extend the contract completion time accordingly. If the owner does not agree with the extension, note this and do not proceed. Keeping the original materials quoted as part of the calculated allowance should be less work and less complicated because you know ahead of time what "typical" materials can be used.

Modifications. Ensure that you mark up and profit from allowance selections that change during the construction process. Note the price and costs on the change order confirming the allowance selections. State that allowance overages are to be paid in advance at the time the change order is signed and executed. This protects you because it verifies all facts. The owner's signature on the change order authorizes you to proceed.

FIGURE 4.1 Allowance Summary Sheet

Project: Showalter Residence
579 Aspen Meadows Subdivision
5117 Mt. Humphrey View Road
Flagstaff, Arizona 86004

Plans: Karen A. Johnson Architects
Dated 11-5-98; 16 pages

This allowance summary schedule condenses the information detailed in the contract specifications with regard to allowance categories, allowance amounts, and dates by which selections must be completed.

Allowance Item	Allowance Amount	Select by Date
1. Skylight options	$1,335	12-1-98
2. Door hardware	748	3-10-99
3. Appliances	5,783	3-15-99
4. Tile selections	4,660	3-15-99
5. Carpet	6,800	4-15-99
6. Electrical fixtures	5,758	4-15-99

Contractor will summarize in writing final client selections.

All materials, products, and fixtures must be selected and purchased from the contractor-approved vendor list.

Amounts for allowances were calculated after a discussion with the architect and owner about types and quality of products desired. Amounts are offered as a guideline for the owner based on these discussions. Final owner selections will determine the actual amounts spent.

Contractor will add a 25 percent handling fee to any amount exceeding the allowance estimate.

_____   _____
Contractor   Date   Owner   Date

Credits. State that allowance "credits" are to be settled with the next construction draw.

Pricing. Quote retail prices for products. This makes it clean, simple, and profitable when the owner upgrades to more expensive products. Why forego making $5 per yard on a carpet upgrade because the architect stated in the plans that all allowance items are provided at builder cost?

Number and type. Limit the number and type of allowance items in the specifications and contract. Use allowances only as a last resort. The owners might not have been able to select materials before the plans were completed. Encourage them to make final selections before the contract is signed and the job begins.

Warranty. Warranty issues are seldom raised, but a significant potential liability can occur on open-ended selection items that are part of allowances. Ask yourself what liability you are willing to assume and then include language in the contract that holds you harmless when an owner does not follow your advice.

Payments. Fully define allowance payments. State that no items will be ordered, installed, or acted upon until the change order defining all outstanding issues regarding the allowance is signed and returned to the contractor. (See Chapter 5, Write Profitable Change Orders).

Make sure that the contract wording is consistent so that the contract, draw schedule, and specifications all work in conjunction with one another to define how the allowances work.

Use Allowance Change Orders

Before preparing an allowance change order that details how the allowance will be resolved, work out the details. Dot the Is and cross the Ts. Note disclaimers, warranty issues, and special circumstances on the change order to minimize disputes and second thoughts.

Use the change order as a checklist to reconfirm the accuracy of the information. Is freight included? What about shipping insurance, delays, wrong orders, malfunctions, etc.? Much of this seems so obvious that it can be settled by common sense, but owners often become narrow-minded when it comes to their personal selections on their very personal, customized home.

Do not do any work until it is agreed to in writing, signed, and allowance overages are paid for in advance.

Protect Yourself

Sometimes an owner wants to eliminate an allowance category to save money, spend that amount on other items, or just eliminate it altogether. Do not put yourself in the position of issuing a full credit for an allowance item to an owner, unless you can do it without costing yourself money, effort, or time.

Under no circumstances should you allow an owner to hire someone else to complete the allowance item while you are still constructing the home. An approved supplier and subcontractor list is a lifesaver in this circumstance.

In the likely event that architects or others stipulate the terms of the allowances, it is up to you to be professional and forthright about the accuracy of the definition of the allowance. Your professionalism will be noted by the owner, architect, appraiser, banker, decorator, subcontractors, suppliers, and everyone else involved with the project. Noting a potential problem at the beginning of the project demonstrates your organization and management skills.

Allowance overrides can cost you time and money without the proper management. My recommendation is to avoid allowances at all costs. Try to get the owners to decide before the project begins.

If you must assign allowances on a project, keep the number to a minimum. Use them as a last resort. Use as few as possible. Trying to close the deal without defining all the selections is the same as a child who says "I'll do my homework later."

Evaluate the Project

A custom home project with numerous (30+) allowance items is really a cost plus contract job. Without calculated allowances, the project probably will be one long seesaw negotiation about costs, schedules, quality of subcontractors, etc. Save your time and effort for an owner that will appreciate and expect the kind of quality and professionalism that your company can bring to their custom home project. A troublesome project with an undefined scope often takes valuable time away from other good projects and owners.

I have pulled out of the running for some custom home projects because so many details were left undefined. A custom home project with 10, 20, or 30 allowances is not a good starting point for a successful end product.

Being the last link in the chain, the builder must pull together all facets of the project and construct a custom home. This is a difficult task at best and near impossible when the owners are unsure of what they want during the project's design phase. The owners' inability to make decisions could be a warning sign of things to come.

5

Write Profitable Change Orders

A custom home by definition will be continually "customized" by architects, owners, and contractors (due to design problems or code compliance adjustments) until the day the project is completed. It is highly unlikely that all decisions and selections made during the design process will hold, especially when a custom home project takes 8 to 12 months or more to complete. People and their priorities change over time.

Because of the constantly evolving nature of custom homes there always will be change orders. Projects that have several active parties involved in making decisions could have as many as 100 or more change orders.

To make a profit on a custom home project, it is essential that you make a profit on change orders. Also use change orders to assign responsibility and the related costs to others, and to protect your schedule and completion dates.

Do change orders make or break your company? Adopt methods outlined here to generate income, while improving project management. Change orders are a key communication tool between owner and contractor.

Calculate Your Costs

Change orders are an excellent source for making money. Think of change orders as a profit center. The owner is requesting that your company do additional work. Your contract language ensures that outsiders cannot do the work, so the requested change must be managed, coordinated, and supervised by your company.

A custom home project that begins with a completion estimate of 11 months and ends up taking 15 months due to changes, dramatically impacts your overhead and profitability. You must obtain compensation for the additional four months of extended work one change order at a time.

When calculating the costs of every change order, include:

- Material and labor costs

- Sales tax, insurance, and additional inspections and permits

- Your company's overhead costs on an hourly or daily basis

- The risks involved with the change, including warranty exposure

- The money you might lose when your workers are pulled off another project (late fees, overtime to accomplish both tasks)

- The difference in the profit that would be generated if your workers were doing other work (does another job provide a 20 percent profit while this project only provides 10 percent?)

- A reasonable profit percentage.

A change order "rule of thumb" is cost plus 100 percent, though for larger changes a 25 to 40 percent markup might be appropriate. Adjust the cost of the change order to reflect the work being done.

All change orders are a cost item unless they merely clarify information. To protect yourself from numerous "what-if" change orders, stipulate in your contract a minimum change order fee—usually $75 to $125. You can waive the fee or apply it. Garnering a return of $100 to $125 on simple changes will probably just cover your overhead. Once the owner spends $500 on whimsical "what-if" questions, either their budget or common sense will prevail. Your goal is to convince the owners that time is money.

Never price change orders onsite. Your verbal estimate will only lead to problems. "You told me that the new skylight would only run $200. Why is this written change order $475?"

Think through the change order and price it back at your office. You need to consider the remodeling, demolition, time delay, special order materials lag time, labor, materials, and ultimately, what other work will not be done while your time and effort is devoted to the change order.

Pricing and enforcing your change orders is simple. When a customer at a car dealership asks the service shop to "add a tune up" to the service order, does the service department argue over the cost or do it for what another dealer would charge? Absolutely not. They inform the client of the price and then ask yes or no? Once you know your overhead costs, it's easy to enforce your pricing. Use contract language, such as the following, to back you up.

> Changes during the progress of work are based on costs of materials, labor, and inherent delays caused by changes during the completion phase. Costs for changes might be influenced by the overall impact on the timely completion of the project.
> Price quotes for change orders are non-negotiable. Individual change orders will document the work to be completed, accompanied by model numbers, colors, sizes, etc., to clarify the work to be completed.

Use as a Management Tool

On each job there is a precedent setting moment that occurs when the owner requests the first change order. Set the mood for the remainder of the job by following the professional and organized procedures you discussed with the owner and put in the contract. The owner will expect change orders to be written up, paid for, and executed only after the document is signed.

A change order is a fundamental management tool for the custom home builder because it documents information at a specific point in the con-

"Here's change order #17 asking that the kitchen be 10 feet wider & change order #4 authorizing a thicker footing!

struction process. The change order becomes an historical record when both the contractor and owner sign, indicating agreement with the change on a specific date. This information is an invaluable way to keep facts straight over an extended period of time.

Track change orders with a change order summary that records the number of the change order, the date, and a brief description. A sample change order summary is provided in Figure 5-1.

Always have the owner/client sign and date each change order. Signed change orders are the only proof you have documenting a change, problem, or delay. Without a signed change order and full payment before work commences, you take a substantial risk that you will not receive payment in full for the job.

If an owner will not sign a change order, do not implement the change. Signed change orders without payment should not be begun until payment is received. When an owner does not agree with a change order such as a weather delay, write up a change order anyway. Make a note on the change order that the owner would not sign it. Note that it was delivered in a timely fashion.

Even one of our country's founding fathers and past presidents faced a change order detailing some of the work that took place at his home, Monticello, during one phase of the constant remodeling that occurred over a 40-year period.

FIGURE 5.1 Change Order Summary

Smith Residence

Lot 79—Apple Blossom Development

123 Apple Orchard Drive

C.O. #	Description	Cost	Date	Delay
1	Make footings 12-inch concrete at rear of home	$640.00	10/6/98	2 days
2	Add underslab conduit for computer tie-in	$125.00	10/6/98	1 day
3	Use fibermesh concrete 3,000 psi in floors	$500.00	10/6/98	0 days

Current Change Order Total: $1,265.00

Date: 10-7-98

Original Completion Date: 6-15-99

New Completion Date: 6-18-99

Original Contract Amount: $325,300.00

New Contract Amount: $326,565.00

"May 15, agreed with Mr. Moore that he shall level 250 f. square on top of the mountain at the N.E. end by Christmas, of which I am to give 180 bushels of wheat, and 24 bushels of corn, 12 of which are not to be paid until the corn comes in. If there should be any solid rock to dig we shall leave to indifferent men to settle that part between us."

(*Jefferson's Monticello*, by William Howard Adams, Abbeville Press, New York, NY; 1985.)

In the above example, Jefferson had to pay extra for some rock to be removed. This is a good example of why a rock clause should be included in every contract.

Use change orders to note any changes that impact the cost, detailing, delays, or decorator specifics required to complete the project. Change orders that clearly define the modification and resulting costs and conditions help minimize disagreements and keep the project moving toward completion. Case Study #5-1 demonstrates how change orders can settle disputes and keep draw payments on schedule.

Write a change order to document any and all information concerning the project that is not contained in either the plans or specifications. Use

CASE STUDY #5.1

Use Change Orders

While the Smith residence was being drywalled, the owners were asked to confirm the interior paint color. They reconfirmed the color without a change. The owners, however, did request that the drywall texture be omitted from several bathrooms so that it would be easier for the owner to later wallpaper those rooms. A change order was prepared and signed by all parties.

At the final owner—builder walkthrough, the owners informed the bank inspector that they wanted the walls smooth for wallpaper and the ceilings textured. The bank inspector made note of the problem and held up the draw for 15 days. The bank inspector was following bank rules that defined the bathrooms "incomplete" due to lack of wall texture and wallpaper. Because the bank funded twice monthly this problem caused the builder to miss the mid-month funding cutoff.

Resolution: The dispute was quickly settled when the builder produced the signed change order that noted the walls were to be left smooth without drywall texture so that the owners could wallpaper in the future.

change orders to track changes and costs added to the original contract amount; document dates; and verify information (model numbers, colors, allowances, etc.), as well as any other actions that effect the project.

There are three types of change orders: confirming or clarifying, time-and-materials, and open-ended. Each is briefly described below.

Confirming or clarifying. These change orders confirm the information in the plans and specifications or put in writing a conversation. You also can use them to answer an owner's questions and to provide progress reports for the project. An owner signing such paperwork documents that the contractor raised the issue, it was resolved, agreed to, and acted upon based on the information in the change order. Below are four examples of different reasons for preparing a confirming or clarifying change order.

> **Example #1:** Owner had mentioned to contractor several weeks ago that he might want to change the texture of the concrete floor located at rear patio #3, which is to be finished per plans and specs with a broom finish. Owner was considering a "Light Rock Salt" finish. As of 3-18-98, owner has given direction to keep the broom finish at patio #3. Cost change: $0. No additional time required.

> **Example #2:** Carpet allowance is outlined in the contract specifications as Franklin Carpet Company, #395 "Whispering Galaxy," plush, nylon carpet with a 3/8-inch rebond pad (density 0.43). Quantity: 290 yards. Vendor: Bingham Bros. Carpet Co., Dallas, TX. Owner's selection: #395 "Whispering Galaxy" in color Saturn Tan with the standard pad. Cost change: $0. No additional time required.

> **Example #3:** On April 8, 1998 the jobsite was hit with an unusual snowstorm that left about 8 inches of new snow. Contractor has scheduled concrete driveway to be installed between April 10 and 15. Contractor has delayed pour due to snow and frigid conditions. Freezing temperatures would damage the quality of the concrete pour and the finish of the concrete. Driveway pour is paramount and will impact the completion schedule for the home. Contractor is notifying owner per this document of a 10-day delay in completion date. Contractor will absorb overhead costs of delaying the project for that period. Cost change: $0. Additional time required: 10 days.

Example #4: Building permit allowance was $2,000 as per contract specifications. Building permit amount was actually $2,947. The City of Irving Building Department was in the process of implementing the new permit fee schedule per the recently adopted 1997 UBC and fees could not be determined at the time of plan submittal. Cost change: $947.00; sales tax and miscellaneous fees included. No additional time required.

Time-and-materials. These change orders note a deviation or alteration from the plans and specifications or scope of work. They include the original specification and the change, plus the cost of the change and the extra time required to make the change. Figure 5-2 is an example of a time-and-materials change order.

The owner has requested that bedroom #4 be painted with 2 coats of PPG 4592 "Georgia Peach," flat, acryllic enamel. Woodwork is to remain stained and lacquered (as per plans/specs.). Cost change: $275.00 + #31.75 (sales tax) = $306.75. No additional time is needed.

Open-ended. Sometimes details are unavailable when a change is discussed, so costs and pricing are difficult to calculate. Avoid this situation if at all possible. Try to employ the logic: "How can I document your requested change when we're still lacking details?" If there really isn't any other way out of the circumstance, state the financial information so that you are protected and your company makes money.

The owner has indicated a desire to change the flooring in the dining room, but is unsure of material and finish. This change order acknowledges that owner desires to make change. Contractor will make change with following parameters:

1. Material costs are at retail price. Labor costs are at quoted price dependent on materials and finish selected. Sales tax will be added on the total price. No additional inspection fees are anticipated.

2. Supervision of change will be made by project superintendent at the rate of $75 per hour or portion thereof.

3. Contractor will total all costs and add 25 percent for overhead and profit.

FIGURE 5.2 Change Order Example

ABC Contracting, Inc.
1500 Johnson Ave.
Dallas, TX 77093

CHANGE ORDER NUMBER: 5

SUBJECT: Propane rank relocate per building inspector.

BASE CONTRACT AMOUNT: $480,000.00

CO #5 COST CHANGE: $1,680.10

REVISED CONTRACT AMOUNT: $482,933.85

PROJECT:	Smith Residence
LOCATION:	Lot 7, Rolling Hills Estates 1572 Rolling View Vista Ave. Irving, Texas 77092
DATE REQUESTED:	3-28-98
REQUESTED BY:	John Johnson, ABC Contracting, Inc.
EXPIRATION DATE:	3-31-98 5:00 PM

DETAILS: Propane tank as noted on plans is not permissible per Jack Timmon, building inspector, Irving, Texas. Tank must be located a minimum of 100 ft. from the residence and 50 ft. away from the street.

Inspector has suggested a new location. Owner has approved that new location, but there will be additional costs for trenching and a gas line of an additional 110 linear ft. Contractor requested the inspector review the propane tank location before it was installed to avoid a more expensive problem.

SUBCONTRACTOR: N/A

VENDOR: N/A

COST CHANGE: $1600.00 + $80.10 (sales tax) = $1,680.10

CONTRACTOR: _____   OWNER: _____

Date: _____   Date: _____

Decision to be made no later than: 12/8/98

Estimated cost: $3,750

Additional time required: minimum 10 days

Owner will sign change order detailing the actual flooring material and finish, with actual cost before work proceeds.

Write Effective Change Orders

Write and document change orders keeping in mind a future discussion with the client that might begin: "Well, I assumed that the _____ would be changed also."

Effective change orders include all pertinent details. Assumptions have no place in change orders. The more information you provide, the better. Be clear, direct, and accurate. Verify brands, model numbers, finishes, colors, textures, sizes, etc.

Make the information "owner friendly" by using model numbers and a common description of the product selected. Most owners cannot distinguish Model 5159 from Model 5160. Describe the components. This is a fail-safe system because if the model number is correct, but upon review the client notes a discrepancy—"We wanted the elliptical sink, not the pedestal sink"—then the correction can be made.

It also is in your best interest to describe product care if inappropriate care might affect your warranty obligations. Case Study #5-2 illustrates how specifying product care absolved a builder's warranty responsibility.

Review the change order for accuracy before you present it to the client. Photocopy information and attach it to the change order. The more information present, the better off and better protected you'll be.

Change orders impact five areas of the contract: completion date, contract amount, payments, specifications, and warranty. Address each of these areas on every change order, even if you write $0 or not applicable.

Completion date. The time factor is the most important aspect of the change order. The time component must include the additional time needed to complete the task and the downtime experienced to replan and reschedule what was already on the calendar. The time extension noted on the change order could be worth its weight in gold when it comes down to completing the project. Adding incorrect or an insufficient amount of time can cost you dearly when you are trying to meet a completion date.

CASE STUDY #5.2

Include Product Care in Your Specifications

A custom home was completed two years past. The contractor receives a phone call from an owner demanding that his tarnished, scratched, and faded hardware needed to be replaced as a warranty item. To replace the polished brass door hardware and plumbing trim would run approximately $12,000.

The contractor visits the home and reviews the situation. He discovers that the owner's new cleaning service personnel had been scrubbing the hardware with a powdered cleaner and a scrubbing pad. The finish had been scratched, buffed out, and damaged on nearly every piece of polished brass hardware in the home.

Resolution: The contractor empathized with the owner, but went back to the contract and specifications. Those documents spelled out the care for hardware and plumbing finishes. Only a soft cloth and water were to be used for said cleaning. The issue was dropped. Just a few words in the specifications can save builders lots of time and trouble.

The additional time and cost of the change order are non-negotiable, as stated in the contract language. The owner must approve or cancel the change order in a timely fashion. Always include an expiration date/cancellation date for the change order. This is a polite reminder to the owner that they have an adequate window to sign and execute the change without causing a major disruption to the scheduling and forward progress of the project. "I need to think about it," is acceptable for three days, not three weeks.

Contract amount. The minimum fee for a change order must cover work items; the time and effort you put into the change order considering

what else you could be doing; a profit percentage; and the amount needed to cover warranty work.

Anytime a change is initiated there is a domino effect. Changing one switch to a dimmer is not a big deal until you consider the timing. Does the electrician have to make a special trip? How much time will this consume on the part of the superintendent or general contractor? Is it a $99 electronic dimmer?

Payments. Always receive full payment for a change order before you begin the work. You take a substantial risk that you will not receive payment if you do not collect up front.

Specifications. A change order most likely will alter the specifications in the contract. Make detailed reference to the specifications and how they change because of the change order.

Warranty. Before you price a change order, consider your warranty exposure. Does the change have the potential to increase your warranty costs? If the change is not consistent with your recommendations, will you still provide a warranty? State specifically any changes in the warranty brought about by the change and include an amount sufficient to cover your exposure in the future. Limit your exposure by noting warranty issues on the change order form.

Track Change Orders

A word processing program is the simplest way to track change orders because the original document is saved and edited with updated changes. The information you need is the date, specific change, time added or deleted, cost of the change, and date approved by the owner.

Documenting changes is part of the organizational skills needed to be a general contractor. Performing in the trade aspect is only part of the overall job. If the general contractor is organized, a method can be set up to take care of change orders properly. The office personnel, contractor, and superintendent have to act as the team implementing the changes.

6

Control the Specifications

I n today's custom home building environment, builders must have plans and specifications to complete the project within budget and on time. So that there are no costly surprises, the plans and specifications must be accurate.

Regardless of who generates the plans and specifications—architects, designers, design builders, homeowners—the bearer of ultimate responsibility for the finished product is the builder. Therefore, builders need to perform due diligence before entering into a contractual agreement with an owner.

The plans and specs documents should detail the scope of work, or what is and is not included in the project. An accurate set of specifications and plans can be the saving grace of a project. The reality is that rarely is every detail outlined in these documents because of the number of people involved in the process. By the time the plans are submitted to subdivision committees, building departments, etc., for final approval, circumstances and decisions already might have changed for any number of reasons.

Bottom-line profitability is influenced most by the specifications. Write and utilize game rules that control the job, the key players, and the costs.

Protect Yourself with Builder's Specifications

As a custom home builder you should have a standard set of written specifications that you include with each contract, even if your specifications are supplemental to other specs that accompany the plans. (See Appendix A, Sample Set of Specifications.)

"Could you change out that one funny brick at row 31, column 19?"

In your set of specifications outline any gray areas that outside parties might not be aware of, interested in, or concerned with because it is not their responsibility. Builder specifications minimize your risk regarding incomplete and changing details that ultimately are your responsibility to complete.

The specifications you write should reflect the needs, requirements, objectives, methods, and applications endorsed by you, your company, and your subcontractors and suppliers. Your contract should reference your specifications and state that the architectural specifications or plan specifications are supplemental to your company's builder specifications. It is acceptable to use both documents, but your set should be the primary specifications. Be sure that the warranty limitations spelled out in your document override those written by the architect.

As an example, I always include this phrase in my standard set of specifications.

> Products (appliances, electronics, security devices, and other mechanical goods) installed in the home will be limited to the individual warranties as stated by the manufacturer. Labor to identify faulty products and replacement or repair of said products will be at an additional charge and is not part of the contractor's warranty or responsibility.

Write Thorough Specifications

Organize the specs alphabetically and address all the construction categories. For each category, state the details about the products, colors, textures, product limitations, sizes, special concerns, special changes, thicknesses, scope of the work in the category, warranties, etc.

Put yourself in the owner's place and write your specs so that a person unfamiliar with construction can easily understand the information. Every word you include will make you money because the more thorough the plans and specifications, the less time and money you will spend on misinterpretations and corrections.

Go through the architectural specifications and identify what will and will not be followed. Many architectural specs outline warranty information that is binding, but has nothing to do with reality. Perfection is a great concept, but seldom applicable to the cold, hard realties of putting 500,000 pieces of noncompatible materials together to move from an artistic rendering to the finished home.

Follow your specifications to the letter. State that any changes to the specifications after the contract is signed will be detailed with change orders. Do not make verbal changes, adjustments, assumptions, and understandings part of the equation.

Reference change order information by the specification so that you can easily update subcontractors on changes and the impact on their particular area of work.

Writing your own specifications might seem like a monumental task. Before you say you don't have the time or ability to write your own specifications, consider this: Every word you put on paper is going to save you money, eliminate stress, and minimize questions and renegotiations as the project progresses. That alone should make your efforts invaluable. Case Study #6-1 illustrates the value of builder's specifications.

Once your project specifications are completed and loaded onto a word processor, they can be adjusted easily to meet the needs of each custom project. Much of the information contained in the specs will be standard information, so the majority of the work is already completed. Your standard set of specs also will serve as a catalyst to make sure most issues are covered and edited for each new project.

Be Specific

Properly written specifications are a useful management tool for all parties involved in the custom home project.

For a complicated custom home, each category could easily wind up being two to three typed pages in length. Remember, the more specific you are on paper, the smoother your project will go.

Typewritten specifications, summarized alphabetically by category, generate efficiency for the project on all levels. The owner can read and under-

Even When You Are Right, You Could Be Wrong!

A builder was constructing a custom home in a subdivision served by the city's municipal utility company for water and sewer. After the home was approximately 40 percent completed it was time to purchase and hook up the water meter and sewer services.

The builder made out a check in the full amount for a ³/₄-inch water meter service and submitted that payment to the city water department. The city refused the "partial" payment for the new water service stating that the fees for that subdivision were based on 1-inch water meter service. Additional fees of $1,235 were required.

The builder's specifications called for a ³/₄-inch water meter service and identified the fees to be paid as such. Also, the approved set of plans redlined by the city building inspection department made no mention of the required meter service and did not stamp the comments on the plans regarding the service requirements. The city did point out that the submitted plat for the new subdivision included a city requirement that all new meters be of the larger 1-inch capacity.

Resolution: The builder submitted a change order to the owner that was signed and paid. It is not the builder's job to review the subdivision plat map that was used for planning and zoning approval. No mention of this meter service was indicated in the covenants, codes, and restrictions for the subdivision. The specifications saved the builder $1,235.

stand the specifications better than reading, scanning, and reviewing the blueprints. Subs and suppliers can access the information more readily because the information is user friendly.

Standard 8.5-x-11-inch pieces of paper can be faxed, carried easily, and referred to more easily than bulky blueprints. And the contractor can quickly refer to specialty details and requirements on the specs that might take some searching to find in the plans.

Plans are not uniform. The drafting quality, completeness of the details, and the location of information are just a few of the faults that occur frequently in professional plans. While the electrical pages of blueprints are usually noted as E-1, E-2, etc., and contain electrical notes, this same information might be contained on the site plan, the floor plan, framing plan, etc.

The builder's specifications bring together all this information and put it in a single, easy-to-find location. The electrician can read the electrical category in the builder's specifications to find out the supplemental information.

Specifications grow and become complicated because of the variety of choices offered to the owner for electrical fixtures and numerous other products. The special applications, installation needs, and limitations of some of these consumer goods are staggering and difficult to keep up with. Ultimately you are responsible for all the products and gadgets included in the project. It is to your advantage to have all the information in a central location.

The best way to explain the detail I believe needs to be in specifications is by example. Several brief examples of builder's specifications follow. A complete set of sample specifications is included in Appendix A. Read the examples and adjust the information so that it makes sense for your company, your circumstances, and your custom projects. Once you have a standard set of specifications, tailor it to meet the needs of individual projects.

Appliances
Appliance warranty is limited to that of the manufacturer. Labor to replace faulty or defective units will be at an additional charge.

- Compactor: None

- Cooktop: General Electric JGP 641 ES (4 burner, gas, white)

- Cooktop vent: General Electric JXDV 66 (white)

- Dishwasher: General Electric 1430 TWW (white)

- Disposal: Insinkerator "Badger V" 1/2 HP unit

- Microwave/convection oven: General Electric JET 344 (white) with trim kit

- Oven: General Electric JKP 45 WP (dual cleaning, wall ovens, white)

- Refrigerator: Subzero 570 (48" wide, dual door freezer/refrigerator)

- Panels (2) to match cabinetry

Driveway
All exterior concrete will be poured to a depth of 6 inches. Plans call for 4 inches. Extra thickness will provide longevity due to harshness of climate and daily temperature fluctuations during the winter months.

Note: Using any ice melting chemicals, heating equipment, or rough, abrasive snow removal equipment or methods will damage the long-term strength of the concrete finish and void all warranty concepts and understandings regarding concrete appearance.

- Driveway finish: Broom finish (no added color).

- Stamped finish concrete (as per plans) was deleted 1-13-98 per owners.

- Layouts remain unchanged.

Concrete will be formed and placed as per plans. Material will be supplied by United Metro (Tanner Concrete) and be of minimum strength 2,500 psi at 28 days.

Contractor may at its discretion use one or more of the following concrete reinforcement materials: nylon/fiberglass fibermesh, 610 welded wire mesh, or steel rebar for additional strength performance.

Pouring of the driveway concrete is planned on the construction schedule, but timing is at the discretion of contractor based on weather, curing periods, access to the site, etc.

Heavy vehicle traffic is not allowed on the driveway for 10 days after pour is completed.

Electrical Fixtures

All fixtures are to be selected and purchased at the Light House, Flagstaff, Arizona, at retail prices. Prices noted above are the contractor's best estimate as to what the owner may spend on certain fixture selections. Bulbs and other necessary trim items will be charged against the overall value of the electrical fixture allowance. Contractor will not install or warrant owner provided fixtures.

- Total allowance: $6,495

- Dining room fixture: $1,500

- Recessed cans: (40) x $38 per can = $1,520

- Exterior entry sconces: (6) x $125 per fixture = $750

- Bulbs needed: $300

- Ceiling fans: 5 x $250 per fan/blades/pole/rheostat = $1,250

- Bedroom 3: $500 (for track lights)

- Study ceiling fixture: $225

- Exterior floodlights: 9 x $50 per fixture = $450

Items charged to allowance: All electrical fixture items including recessed cans, recessed can trim, bulbs, and interior and exterior fixtures.

- Recessed cans: Juno IC 22 (6-inch diameter up to 75 watts of light)

- Recessed can trims: Juno Eyeball #229 (white) for vaulted and soffit-ted ceilings; Juno Black Baffle #24 (black) for flat ceilings

- Plugs, switches and cover plates: Leviton brand, standard toggle style, ivory color, standard-style switches and plugs. Other colors are optional.

Note: Wiring, switches, plugs, bath fans, and breaker box are not part of this allowance item.

Floor Coverings
The total floor covering allowance is $18,685. Included in this figure are the following areas of the home:

- Carpeted areas: living, family, rec room, all bedrooms, guest room, Dan's office, upper hallway, both sets of stairs

- Tile flooring: kitchen, breakfast nook, sunroom, laundry, powder room, bar, kids' bath 1, kids' bath 2

- Vinyl flooring: mudroom

- Wood flooring: none

Carpet selection: _____

Tile selection (floor only): _____

Vinyl floor selection: _____

Carpet selection. Carpet is to be supplied and ordered from Bing Bros. Carpet Co. Prices quoted are based on floor covering use per plans. Carpet waste, pad, and installation labor may change based on actual carpet selection. Allowance calculation assumes a plush carpet over 9/16-inch standard rebond pad. Prices will be quoted to owner; order will be verified with a signed change order. Carpet is based on Mohawk "Melody River" which comes in 17 colors and 12-foot rolls.
Calculations:

- 4,310 sq. ft. × 6% percent waste = 4,569 sq. ft.

- 4,569 sq. ft./9 sq. ft. per sq. yd. = 508 sq. yds.

- 508 sq. yds. × $30 per yd. = $15,240

Tile selection. Included in the calculations is the labor charge for standard floor tile and the grout cost using standard C-Cure colors.
Calculations:

- 355 sq. ft. × 10 percent waste = 391 sq. ft. tile

- 400 sq. ft. (tile ordered in 10 sq. ft. boxes)

- 400 sq. ft. × $8 per sq. ft. = $3,200

Vinyl selection. Vinyl roll width and pattern or layout could impact the amount of vinyl needed for a specific room.
Calculations:

- 110 sq. ft. × 9 sq. ft. per sq. yd. = 12.2 sq. yds.

- 12.2 sq. yds. × $20 per sq. yd. = $245

7

Use Your Own Contract

The basis for making money in the custom home construction industry is a detailed, complete, and understandable contract. The more understandable the contract, the easier it is to follow and enforce.

Make every word in your contract count; avoid lots of legalese. Prepare your contract with the help of a licensed, authorized legal representative familiar with the building industry.

Your contract is key to ensuring your potential for profitability. Consider these key points.

- A contract that the builder and owner can read and understand is essential. Keep the legal wording to a minimum.

- Use your own contract. Stay away from owner or architect contracts. They protect everyone involved except you.

- Type your contract on a computer and customize it for every job and changing circumstances.

Contract wording and character sets the tone for business interaction among the custom home team. Make sure your contract contains language that is understood by everyone and protects your interests.

■ Use the same standard contract over and over. Familiarity with the language gives you the confidence to stand behind your requirements for specifications, schedules, allowances, change orders, and draws.

Develop an Inclusive Document

An inclusive contract is in reality multiple documents. The main contract includes by reference the architect's plans and specifications. Addendums to the contract should include detailed information in three categories: allowances, draw schedule, and builder specifications.

"My lawyer says 10 months is too long for a custom home!"

Allowances. Allowances create more work for the contractor. My best advice is to keep allowances to a minimum. If you must include allowances follow the suggestions in Chapter 4, Make Allowances a Profit Center

Draw schedule. Include the draw schedule, amounts of each draw, and clearly defined requirements about what must be completed before a draw is paid. (See the sample draw schedule in Chapter 8, Prepare a Custom Draw Schedule.)

Builder specifications. Owners have a difficult time reading blueprints and blueprint details, but most are comfortable with written specifications. Even if specs accompany the plans, make sure you also include your own set of specifications as part of the construction bid. A well written set of specs can save you bundles of money, time, and heartache once the project starts.

Both the owner and contractor should sign and date the plans and specifications, as well as the contract and its addendums. Retain the signed copies for reference purposes.

Protect Yourself

Your contract protects you; it looks out for your best interests. Spell out your role in relation to others involved in the project, such as the owner, architect, bank, and designer. Clarify that you work for the owner—not the architect or designer.

With your custom home contract you put forward not only your price, but also the terms and conditions under which you agree to take on the project.

Your contract should include a written policy that allows you to substitute like items in the event a product is unavailable at the time it is needed. This clause could save you time and help you avoid costly delays, both of which are vital to maintaining your profit margin. An example of the wording I use is:

> Due to changes and availability of both manmade and natural products, materials, colors, updated building codes, etc., the contractor reserves the right to substitute products or materials of equal value and similar appearance to those goods specified for this project.

Your contract also should state that you are not responsible for correcting plan mistakes, guessing at dimensions, and making field adjustments based on what will and will not go together. (See Chapter 9, Assign Responsibility for Mistakes.)

Address the fact that mistakes and omissions in the plans will occur and outline the steps that are to be taken to resolve them. Errors in the plans can require costly corrections, generate inaccurate subcontractor bids, and result in costly delays. Address the potential costs of such delays as a monetary issue before they occur.

If an owner or architect insists on a completion penalty, you should insist on an incentive clause that amounts to several times the amount they requested in the delay clause. It only makes sense that if the time element is important, then the reward element should be equally important. A builder can make lots of work happen by funding incentive payments and overtime from the early completion reward incentive.

Before you give away your services without a construction contract, negotiate a retainer. Prepare a binding agreement that spells out your compensation. My recommendation is that you define your services and receive payment that ultimately will be charged against the construction contract price. Write this into the contract as a percentage of costs or a fixed dollar amount.

The retainer protects you if the project is cancelled. It also commits the owner to use you as the contractor. Many times, contractors and owners separate at the last minute due to a conflict or disagreement. Owners also have been known to review the primary contractor's bid with another contractor to see if they can get a lower price. The retainer acts as a binder.

Case Study #7.1 illustrates a situation in which the builder should have obtained a retainer before discussing a custom home plan with a potential client.

Another protective measure you can take during the design phase is to stipulate an hourly consultative rate, monthly fee, or salary. That way if the project design and plan completion phases carry on and on, or if the owner selects another builder, you are compensated. Remember, you are a professional. Your time is valuable and you should be compensated even if numerous changes cause delays that really cannot be blamed on anyone or anything in particular.

CASE STUDY #7.1

Have a Rock Solid Contract

A builder met with a potential owner about building a custom home. The owner initially contacted the builder after seeing the builder's sign on another custom residence. The owner informed the builder that he and his wife really liked the home that they had seen, but might want to make some minor changes, select colors, textures, etc. They discussed timing, plans, and overall price.

The meeting concluded and time passed. The builder followed up via telephone with the potential owner, but did not receive encouraging responses. After six months passed, the builder noticed a home in the same subdivision that was similar to the custom home the owner had inquired about. Checking the building department records, the builder found that it was an owner/builder job and the property owner listed was the potential client he had met with previously.

The builder walked through the home during the framing stage and discovered it was nearly identical to the custom home his company had designed and built previously.

He contacted the owner/builder and received no response. After a lawyer contacted the owner/builder, it was confirmed that the home was nearly identical to the builder's custom home.

After much back and forth, the builder filed a criminal complaint with the county attorney. The builder's attorney also filed a mechanic's lien against the property. (Some states do not allow liens on property for professional services rendered such as design, surveying, and engineering.)

Resolution: The owner was arrested and the builder was paid $15,000 for the time, trouble, and copyright infringement on his plans, plus all legal fees and expenses. The builder could have avoided this situation by requesting a retainer from the potential client before talks escalated.

You might scare off some clients with a retainer or monthly fee, but that is okay. Clients who agree demonstrate their commitment to you and to the project. When money changes hands, the commitment begins.

Include Key Issues

A comprehensive contract includes a number of key issues. Listed below are some basic contract categories and information that each should address. The information presented here is for the purposes of discussion and review only. Specific wording should be written or reviewed by your legal representative for accuracy and compliance with local laws, statues, and practices. As with any legal document, proper and accurate information is crucial.

- Owner information: name, address, telephone numbers, fax number, etc.

- Contractor information: name, company, license number, address, telephone numbers, fax number, etc.

- Job description: street address, lot number, subdivision, tax parcel number, lot size, city, county, state, and zip code

- Plans description: architect; architect's address and license number; plan pages; architectural specification pages; dates of plans

- Purpose of the agreement: Outline the reasoning for the agreement and its purpose; state that contract, specifications, allowances, and draw schedules provided by the contractor will override any other documentation both written or understood.

The contract categories listed below are in alphabetical order for reference purposes. They may be included in the contract in a logical order.

Allowances

- Define how the allowances work and how they were determined.

- State that only approved subcontractors and suppliers may be used.

- Define policies, payments, discounts, and pricing.

- Provide the deadline dates on product and decorator selections and how failure to meet these deadlines will affect the project.

- Specify costs for freight, delivery, sales taxes, etc.

- Reference the allowance scope in the appropriate category in the specifications.

- State that allowance selections, details, costs, delivery dates, cancellation policies, special orders, etc., will be documented on the change order for the allowance item(s). Additional costs will be due and payable at the time of execution.

Building permits

- Define how these are applied, obtained, and altered per direction of the building department officials.

- Explain policy on redlines and changes required by others to the bid set of plans.

- Address the possibility that the approved set of plans might require additional work by others at additional expense to the owner.

Change orders

- Explain policies on change orders and how they are prepared, presented, authorized, and paid.

- Define the use and purpose of the change order summary sheet and explain that it will be updated with every change order and revision.

Code compliance

- Define the responsibilities of the architect, inspector, builder.

- Note in your contract the adopted year of the Uniform Building Code (UBC) being followed. Changes to the codes and their interpretations may result in a change order with additional costs for the owner.

Contractor contact person (See builder representative)

Contract period and delays

- Define the amount of time you have to complete the project. Note any potential delays (weather, custom items, etc.). It is better to make all parties aware of potential problems early on, not after the fact.

- Outline your policy describing how delays will be documented and how the owner will be informed.

- Review the deadline dates on product and decorator selections and how noncompliance may delay completion of the project.

- Define the deadline dates and purposes thereof for change orders.

Draw requests

- Outline the payment schedule and procedure.

- Include a draw schedule as part of an addendum to your contract.

- Define the scope of the contract amount and how it will be distributed (10 draws of equal value, etc.).

- Use your company's draw forms; not those provided by the bank or architect.

- Define the time limitations, frequency of draws, role of the bank inspector, etc.

- Explain penalties for delayed draw payments.

Environmental issues

- Define the scope of indoor air quality.

- Define the scope of land (lot) preexisting contamination.

- Define the scope of ground water/geological/soil conditions.

- Define the scope of radon/lead and mineral issues.

Independent contractors, subcontractors, and suppliers

- Explain your policy that only approved personnel are allowed to enter and conduct work on the jobsite.

Independent inspectors

- Define the limitations and policies regarding the owner's use of an independent inspector.

- Explain that no one is allowed onsite until their insurance certificates are on record in the contractor's office.

- Inspector visits should be conducted only when accompanied by a representative of the contractor.

Insurance

- Outline your insurance coverages and limitations.

- Require the owner to carry course-of-construction and fire insurance.

- Require your company to be written onto the owner's insurance policies as a co-insured party.

■ Define the purpose, scope, and limitations on your worker's compensation policy.

■ Define your policy for theft, vandalism, and the financial responsibility for such.

Jobsite general conditions

■ Define how and when cleanup will take place.

■ Outline policies on job noise, dust, parking, employee behavior standards, radios, relatives, visitors, etc.

■ Define how the final cleanup will be done in and around the property; include sidewalk and street cleaning.

■ Define impact warnings on surrounding plant life, soil disturbances, animals, ground water, water runoff and erosion, well contamination, and soil conditions.

■ Define the responsibility for lot staking, marking property corners, mapping topography and its accuracy, etc.

■ Stipulate limitations and disclaimers on building materials (both natural and manmade).

Landowner

■ Verify the name and address of the landowner per county records. Signing a contract with a third party might limit your rights, your ability to sue, and lien options.

■ Identify in the contract the person, company, or financial institution in the first lien position for the project.

■ Write that the contract must be with the landowner, not a third party. Verify the actual landowner via county tax records.

■ State in the contract that it is the owner's intention to occupy the property upon completion.

■ State that the project is being constructed according to residential standards. State that the structure will not be occupied or employed for a nonconforming commercial use.

■ Stipulate that the owner cannot sell or assign the project to a third party during the construction contract period or until post completion. Your warranty is with the original owner, not a third party.

Lien waivers

■ State that you will send a preliminary lien notice (a 20-day notice) to the property owner to confirm the contract terms and to assure compliance with state lien laws.

■ State that the owner should not sign any agreements, contracts, or other paperwork with anyone or any company regarding the project other than the contractor. This protects the owner through the lien rights of the contractor.

■ State that the contractor will provide a lien waiver for the amount of each payment. A blanket lien waiver covers the full amount of the construction draw payment.

■ Explain that you will prelien the project with a 20-day preliminary notice.

Occupancy and final inspection

■ Define how completion of the project is determined. "Final payment is due upon passing the final inspection by the city building department."

■ State that owner occupancy may take place only after the final inspection.

■ Explain that punch list items are limited once the owner occupies the residence.

Builder representative

■ Explain that as the contractor you sign all paperwork and have ultimate responsibility for the project. You will negotiate with the owner and architect or others as needed.

■ Designate one contact person.

■ Specify the times during which the contact person is available: "business hours only, 8-5 p.m."

Owner representative

■ Define one decision maker; one person to sign paperwork.

■ Explain that this person signs the building permit, utility applications, subdivision applications, etc.

■ Indicate that this person minimizes the time you spend with third parties.

■ State that this person signs and authorizes payments, draws, and changes.

■ Clarify that this individual deals with the homeowner association.

Owner storage of materials onsite

■ State that owner may not store materials onsite during the construction period.

■ State that owner's property is not the responsibility of the contractor, its subcontractors, suppliers, or other affiliated tradespeople.

Payments (see draw schedules and change orders)

Plans

■ State that you, the builder, are not responsible for proofreading the plans for the architect.

■ Define the limitations of your responsibilities.

■ Define the responsibilities of the architect, engineer, surveyor, designer, and the interior designer.

■ Explain that others are responsible for the project being compliant with zoning, subdivision rules, setbacks, height restrictions, color restrictions, covenants, codes, and restrictions. As the contractor, you are responsible for completing the work defined by the plans and specifications.

■ Indicate that plans and the expenses associated with that work are the responsibility of the owner. The contractor is responsible for assembly and completion, not for the continuity, structural compliance, and accuracy or aesthetics of the finished selections.

Rock clause (Employ an attorney to write what will work in your area; this is sample wording only.)

■ State that soil conditions may require nontypical excavation methods and equipment that will be at an additional cost. Cost will be documented with a change order.

■ Explain that rock removal will be an additional charge: "Rock removal has not been included as part of the contract or part of the contract pricing."

■ State that your pricing is based on the assumption that the soil conditions will permit the excavation and installation of the designed footing and structural system without additional support or atypical removal. Substandard compaction, erosion, or clay conditions may require additional design, engineering work, excavation, footing support, or miscellaneous work that will result in an additional cost.

Sales and use taxes

■ Define who pays what and when.

■ Outline procedure for unpaid or delayed tax payments.

■ State that you are not responsible or accountable to owner with regard to property taxes, subdivision assessments or fees, value-added taxes, surtax assessments, or deductions for sales taxes (either implied or endorsed).

Specifications

■ State that written contract specifications take precedence over the plans.

■ Reference your builder specifications and acceptable local UBC standards.

■ State that specifications are a good faith effort by the contractor to identify, clarify, and detail selections, colors, choices, and limitations on house phases and components as per the experiences and recommendations of the contractor.

■ Stipulate that any allowance items will be detailed and defined in the specifications part of the contract. Allowance amounts will be calculated to determine an accurate estimate on the finished cost.

Standards (Registrar of Contractors)

■ Note that the construction will be carried out according to the UBC (include the year of the code), along with the minimum standards set forth by the state registrar of contractors office.

■ State that quality of workmanship will be as set forth by the minimum acceptable standards required by the Federal Housing Administration (FHA)/Veterans Administration (VA) and the U. S. Department of Housing and Urban Development (HUD) office.

Subcontractors and suppliers

- State that work must be conducted by subcontractors and suppliers approved by the contractor.

- State that allowance selections will be purchased, installed, and coordinated by an approved subcontractor or supplier designated by the contractor; outside sources may disturb continuity, efficiency, and insurance requirements.

- Explain that subcontractors, suppliers, vendors, and other professionals will not be permitted to conduct work onsite without the express, written permission of the contractor. This is a protection policy to ensure quality for both owner and contractor.

- State that no one is allowed to work on the project until an insurance certificate is provided to the contractor.

Subdivision or design review fees

- Define which party pays for and manages the subdivision or design review phase of the custom home project.

- Define the liaison contact with the design review board.

- Define possible additional fees for contractor involvement with the design review board on changes during the project.

Warranties

- Define your punch list policies—what is and is *not* included. Quote a cost-per-hour figure for nonpunch list repairs or additional work requested by the owner at the time of closing.

- Summarize and list the owner's maintenance responsibilities.

- Define and outline limits and environmental risks of termite protection, bug sprays, and chemical ingredients used during the construction of the home.

- State that due to the variety of materials such as (both natural and manmade) glues and solvents, and the possibility that these products might "off-gas," you recommend to the owner that the home be aired out weekly during the first year of occupancy to maintain air quality within the living areas.

- Define the limitations of the contractor with regard to damage from wind, ice, rain, hail, lightning, sunlight, etc.

- Spell out what is and is not part of the warranty.

- State that you comply with your local and state warranty laws.

- State that technical and mechanical devices are warranted by the manufacturer, not the contractor. Labor fees to correct failures will be at owner's expense.

- Explain limitations with regard to utility connections, service, and activation.

- Provide the statute of limitations on warranty periods per state laws.

- Note limitations on electronic devices and surge protectors.

- State that no verbal or implied warranties exist. All warranties are written only per this contract.

- State that you are not responsible for ultraviolet (UV) protection; the discoloration of fabrics, textures, colors, and finishes; or the fading of paints, stains, and other manmade or natural materials.

- State that window tints, glazes, and coatings void all glazing warranties.

Select a Contract Type

Either the contractor or the client selects the type of construction contract. It is to your benefit to select the type of contract that minimizes your risks, increases the possibility of monetary rewards, and defines clearly in a precise and understandable manner the specifications and terms of the agreement.

The three types of contracts are:

- lump sum

- negotiated price

- cost plus

Each contract type has its own distinct features that must be evaluated against the size, scope, complexity, and timing of the project. Each contract type has both advantages and disadvantages.

Use Lump Sum Contracts

The lump sum contract proposes a single price that covers everything specified for the project. The owner receives a home per the plans and specifications for a guaranteed price. With quality plans and specs, a good builder can make money with this type of contract. The upside is that any money saved during the project goes directly to the builder. The downside is that poor bidding and planning might eventually cost the builder money.

The lump sum contract limits the owner's liability. The contractor's risk of making a profit is a function of his or her management skills, such as bidding, budgeting, scheduling, planning, and following through.

To make money with a lump sum contract, your specifications must detail what is and is not included, what has changed, problems expected, exceptions to the standard warranty on special order items, and other details that define what the owner is to receive.

Be Wary of Negotiated Contracts

Negotiated contracts can place all the responsibility on the contractor, while providing little or no authority. This type of contract has its own place and function, but only under very special circumstances.

Negotiated contracts usually are requested when the owner's desires, building plans, and construction costs are out of sync and there are many open-ended issues and details that lack definition.

Several questions usually accompany a negotiated contract:

- How was the budget determined?

- What about early payment discounts?

- Who resolves payment disputes to subcontractors and suppliers?

- What is the chain of command—the owner or the contractor?

- What sort of record keeping is required?

- Are the bills paid weekly or monthly?

- Who coordinates and approves the bids and estimates from the subcontractors and suppliers?

- Is a budget overrun of 50 percent or 150 percent going to be a problem? Costs are hard to define due to lack of detailing.

- With so many details unresolved, how can the contractor estimate the amount of money or fees to charge the owner?

The owner also might desire a negotiated contract when he or she wants the contractor's responsibilities to be more in line with those of a construction manager than an overall contractor. In this case, a typical negotiated contract is based on the contractor receiving a fixed fee for the entire project. The owner pays for all subcontracted work, supplies, permits, fees, taxes, and miscellaneous expenses as they occur. One of the fundamental flaws with this type of agreement is payment and the timing of payments to keep the work moving forward.

Working with a negotiated contract is time consuming and cumbersome. If you are going to use a negotiated contract, I recommend that you do not give away your time and experience. Request a retainer from the client, in the form of a small percentage of the expected contract or a fixed fee, such as $5,000. That amount will compensate you for the time you spend or it can be applied as a down payment to the final contract amount.

Avoid Cost Plus Contracts

With a cost plus contract you receive a fee based on the overall project costs. Typically, fees range from 10 to 25 percent, depending on how the calculations are defined. Many contractors implement a 20-percent fee schedule (10 percent profit plus 10 percent overhead) for any and all cash costs associated with the construction of the custom home.

Cost plus contracts are confusing, loosely defined, misused, and misunderstood. In short, they are a poor method of providing construction services. Living with a fixed fee, such as 10 percent, might take advantage of either builder or client. Stay away from cost plus jobs and contracts unless you have a proven, profitable track record or you can write a contract that compensates you at 25 percent or more.

Record keeping is the source of all cost plus contract problems. Your accounting must be impeccable or conflicts will occur. If you must use a cost plus contract, there are several ways to organize the calculation methods and definitions. Types 1 and 2 below work best when analyzed for the actual circumstances of the project and client.

Cost Plus #1. Follow these steps:

- Include a monthly overhead figure.

- Include a monthly management or administration fee for the contractor.

- Include those amounts in the cost calculation.

- Then multiply the profit percentage to determine the total fees.

Cost Plus #2. Follow these steps:

- Use a flat percentage for all costs.

- Define wage, salary, hourly fees for your employees, and the work to be conducted.

- Define exclusions, such as permits, sales taxes, utility tap fees, etc., from the calculation amount.

It is difficult to combine cost plus contracts and change orders. Builders and clients generally view the combination of these two documents quite differently. Clients usually assume that the cost plus percentage amount carries through change orders. But to builders, change orders represent more work and thus cost more.

Quote change orders as an additional cost only and use the contract percentage markup plus an administrative fee. This compensates you for the added work. You also can bill hourly for the additional time you spend measuring, revising special orders, reviewing the change with subs, etc. Some changes can easily eat up four to five hours of office time that otherwise could be spent generating income. Make sure you are paid for your efforts.

In my opinion, the best overall contract is the lump sum contract. Use negotiated and cost plus contracts for special jobs and projects and their unique circumstances. If you can use those types of agreements and make money, so be it. My experience is that once you experience a tedious, time consuming, detail-upon-detail negotiated or cost plus project, you will stay away from them.

8

Prepare a Custom Draw Schedule

Historically, the construction business has operated on a 5-draw system. The builder is funded 20 percent of the contract amount at five specific stages of completion. This method is endorsed by banks, title companies, mortgage lenders, appraisers, and others involved in the construction process.

I believe times have outgrown the 5-draw payment system for custom home construction due to a number of reasons. Primarily, the 5-draw system hampers the general contractor's cash flow. An extended construction project that lasts 10 to 12 months or more cannot operate with funding every 8 weeks.

Custom homes require customized draw schedules. If all involved parties work together to develop the draw schedule, everyone benefits. For the owner and financial institution, the draws specify what is to be completed before each draw is funded. Coordinating the completion and draw schedules assures timely payments, usually monthly. A customized draw ensures that funds will be available to pay subcontractors and suppliers quickly to

Custom homes call for customized draw schedules. Learn to employ a simpler, builder favorable payment system to keep the project moving forward.

take advantage of early-pay discounts. Use the cost estimate to line out funding requirements at different phases of construction when preparing your draw schedule.

Use a 10-Draw System

The 10-draw system is a comfortable payment schedule for builders of most high-end custom homes. All draws are 10 percent, with two exceptions. The framing draw is 15 percent and the final draw is 5 percent.

This method is simple. The draws are accompanied by a list of completed items, and the owner or funding institution is only holding 5 percent of the contract amount at job completion. This is more reasonable than having the owner hold the final 20 percent of the contract amount until minor punch list items are completed. See Appendix B, Sample 10-Draw Schedule.

Be specific in your construction contract about how the draws are set up and carried out. Custom homes seem to be plagued with minor adjustments along the way and the last thing you want is a draw request payment withheld because some minor item was not completed. Case Study #8.1 illustrates how your contract can keep payments flowing on schedule.

CASE STUDY #8.1

Enforce Your Contract

A custom home was being built for a professional and his family. The contract was set up with a 10-draw schedule with parameters for each draw thoroughly defined. The contract stated that draws were to be funded within 48 hours of bank inspection. For the first three draws, however, funding usually occurred within 20 days from the time the draw request was submitted to the bank. The bank always had some vague reasons as to why there was a delay.

When the fourth draw was submitted, the builder followed the process closely and again it became apparent that there was a hold up. An investigation showed that the owner had been delaying signing and approving the draw requests as his policy of assuring that more work was completed than had been funded. It was his security system of protecting himself and his financial position. He simply would not go to the bank and sign the request until 20 days had passed. Meanwhile, work progressed on the project.

Resolution: When this became known, the builder issued a letter to the owner and the bank restating the conditions of the contract and that there was no mention of the owner approving draw requests before funding could occur. The future draw requests were received without a delay.

Tailor Your Draw Schedule

I structure my draw schedule according to the following theories.

Minimize the final draw. Usually 5 percent is acceptable for the final draw. You do not want an owner holding 15 to 20 percent of a million dollar project as a hammer against the punch list or other concessions wanted at the last minute. Case Study #8.2 shows how you can minimize the amount held after the sale of a spec house.

Maximize the framing draw. Most projects are slightly overfunded at several draw stages and underfunded during the draw for the most important part of the work—the structure. You might want to set up the draw system in equal draw amounts, except for framing completion, when 15 or 20 percent is acceptable. In less expensive 5-draw contracts, you can stipulate a 35-percent draw at framing completion. Balance the other percentages with the amount and cost of the work being conducted and completed.

Minimize cash outlay risks. Submitting a draw request every three to five weeks is a good communication tool. Once the funding mechanism is in place, the bank and owner will be accustomed to providing funds to you on a tighter time frame. If there are any problems or glitches with withheld funds, they are exposed quickly and your cash outlay risks are held to a minimum.

Customize the draw schedule for each project. Review your cash requirements while the project is progressing and set up your draw schedule

---

CASE STUDY #8.2

Minimize the Amount Held

XYZ Builders was constructing a spec home that was 80 percent complete. A buyer approached the builder and wanted to purchase the home, with the addition of several customized finish items that would be completed after the home closed. After negotiations back and forth, the builder agreed to the sale with change orders documenting all changes. The change orders were paid for in advance.

The escrow company was instructed to hold 5 percent of the sales price as a retainer until all change orders were satisfactorily completed. The 5-percent retainer was to be paid within three days of the change orders being completed. The remaining funds were issued to the builder even though the home was only 80-percent complete.

Resolution: The home was sold, change orders funded, and the only amount of money at risk for the builder was 5 percent of the sales price.

to follow that pattern. A 10-percent, 10-draw system can be altered easily to 12-percent or 15-percent draws spaced out to reflect higher cash outlays to accommodate certain phases of the work.

Request a down payment. A down payment to the builder, at the time of contract execution, is an industry standard. Usually that amount is $5,000 to $25,000 and is charged against the first draw. As an example: Draw #1 is 10 percent on a $1,200,000 custom home contract. The down payment of $25,000 is charged against $120,000. In cash terms, Draw #1 is funded at $95,000. Other names you can use for the down payment are retainer or contract binder.

When you sell a spec house, make sure the earnest money is of sufficient size to compel the buyers to settle. Once you have the check—deposit it! Case Study #8.3 illustrates how the earnest money can save the sale at closing time.

List substitutes for incomplete category items. There has hardly ever been a project that proceeded exactly as planned or synchronized. Be prepared and aware of this. Use wording in the draw schedule to

CASE STUDY #8.3

Make Sure Earnest Money Is Sufficient

ABC Builders constructed a spec home in a resort community. The home was 95 percent complete when the buyers and seller agreed on a sales contract for $395,000. The builder made several minor concessions to the buyers as part of the sales price. The buyers requested several additional items that were not completed because they were not in the sales contract and the buyers did not sign the additional change orders.

Several weeks later, the home was completed and passed inspection. On closing day, the buyers inspected the residence with the real estate agent and gave their tacit approval of the finished home.

On closing day at the title company, three parties were present: buyers, seller, and real estate agent. The buyers reviewed the closing papers and refused to sign them because they thought the real estate agent's sales commission was too high (5 percent for a total of $19,750). The buyers then informed all parties that unless the real estate agent agreed to pay for the additional changes, they would refuse to sign until the commission was reduced by $10,000.

Resolution: The title officer left the room and returned several minutes later with the title company's lawyer. The lawyer quickly explained that the commission was agreed to in several sales contract documents that the buyers had signed previously. The buyers had placed $25,000 in an escrow account. The lawyer explained that if the buyers chose to cancel the sale and not sign the final closing contract, they would forfeit their $25,000. After several minutes, the buyers signed the closing papers and the title company funded checks to the bank, real estate agent, and builder.

allow substitutes. Using language that allows for an exchange of completion items is commonly done and expected, but you need to discuss this procedure ahead of time with the funding person or entity to avoid problems.

Prepare a written summary for the bank inspector stating what work has been completed and what work is lacking. Make note of other completed work that is part of upcoming draws that you would like to exchange for the incomplete categories. This demonstrates effective management. It also provides documentation for the inspector's records indicating the reasons for funding the draw request and adjustments.

Define the role, function, and authority of the bank or draw inspector. Define the role of the person in charge of approving your draw request. State the time requirements, such as when the draw is to be funded. Waiting 10 days because the owner is out of town or the inspector is on vacation and cannot approve the request is unacceptable. Case Studies #8.4 and #8.5 demonstrate why the role, function, and authority of the bank are important to receiving timely payments.

Use your own draw schedule. The American Institute of Architects' (AIA) draw schedule forms are straight forward and acceptable for commercial projects, but they seldom fit the needs of custom home builders. For the most part, the AIA forms require that you complete categories and line items, each of which has a value attached. If the categories are

---

CASE STUDY #8.4

Once Authorized Time to Pay

The draws for a custom home were funded by the bank. Draw requests were approved via a 10-draw schedule. A bank inspector reviewed the work items and approved the quality and completeness of the work before funding could occur. The bank officer approved the draws, but would not fund them until the owner came into the bank and authorized the draws.

Every time a draw was submitted for funding, the owner used his approval as a leverage to negotiate concessions from the builder. It became apparent that the owner's strategy was to authorize a draw only after the builder adjusted the pricing on a specific change order, performed changes for no additional costs, or waived the fees on other proposed changes.

Resolution: The builder got a lawyer to review the draw schedule and approval process with the bank. Only then were the draws funded within several days of being approved. The lawyer reviewed the situation with bank officials, who in turn explained to the owner that there is a legal difference between negotiation and extortion.

CASE STUDY #8.5

Find a Way to Make the System Work

One owner built a custom home using a 5-draw contract scenario. The base contract amount was $600,000. The owner found it very painful to write checks for $120,000; draws were often delayed. The builder politely called and asked for the payment to no avail. The builder then requested that the architect, who had approved the draw request, intervene or work was going to stop until payment was made. Payments resumed.

Resolution: Have funds paid through a third party, such as a trust company or title company. This is also a perfect example of why monthly draws or a 10-draw payment schedule works better than a 5-draw schedule. It is less painful for an owner to authorize or write checks monthly for smaller amounts.

not outlined correctly, confusion might cause payment delays. My advice is to use your draw schedule. Write it based on your needs and your funding requirements.

Define the work parameters. State the work parameters as clearly as possible in your draw request form. Make sure that the form is part of the contract documents to assure smooth sailing. Working out some of the details with the architect or financial institution ahead of time also might make matters easier. With experience, your draw schedule will define itself.

Evaluate past projects and cash requirements. Review your previous projects that were similar. Critique what went well and where improvement is needed. Did you delay paying subcontractors or suppliers? As a subcontractor or supplier, where would your priorities be—with a contractor who pays within five days of work completion or one who pays 30 days or more after you are finished? The answer is obvious. To keep good subcontractors you need to pay them in a timely manner. Arrange your draws so that you are able to do so.

Separate Draw Requests and Change Orders

Change orders are always funded at the time of signature and owner approval. You can adjust this to avoid receiving several checks over several days from the owners, but keep to the requirement that all change orders are paid before the work starts.

From experience, I keep draw requests and change orders independent of one another. I have been involved with several projects, however, that have had more than 125 change orders, some of which were funded several at a time and even monthly.

9

Assign Responsibility for Mistakes

Custom homes are more complicated than the average American tract home built for today's market. Architects and designers often edit the floor plans, elevations, and other documents several times as the owners customize their "dream home."

Inevitably, this process generates mistakes and oversights that are difficult to detect until the project moves from two-dimensional paper plans to a three-dimensional home.

To protect yourself and your bottom line, state in your contract that it is not your responsibility to correct plan mistakes, guess at dimensions, and make field adjustments based on what will and will not go together.

Address these mistakes and omissions in the plans in your contract. Develop procedures that are to be taken to resolve them. Errors in the plans can require costly corrections, generate inaccurate subcontractor bids, and result in costly delays. Include policies that cover your costs and your profit percentage. Case Study #9.1 illustrates how your contract wording can resolve disputes.

Mistakes, errors, and omissions cost everyone money. Techniques outlined here assign responsibility where it belongs. Keep problems caused by outside influences from eroding your profits by minimizing your exposure and expenses.

CASE STUDY #9.1

Make Notes, Notes, Notes

Window casing and apron trim detail was not on the plans drawn by a licensed architect. The contract category addressing missing details on plans covered the builder because it made note of this. The builder's specifications referenced in the builder's contract also addressed the fact that there was a gaping hole in the window trim details. The architect and owner got together and shared the opinion that the builder was irresponsible for signing a contract without detailing and including the cost for the window casework.

Resolution: The builder noted the problem in a change order during the drywall phase so that the issue could be resolved in a timely manner. Contract language was referred to that stated the builder was not responsible for correcting plan mistakes. The procedures in the contract were followed and the issue was resolved.

Provide for Compensation

Just as many owners and architects insist on completion penalties, your contract should reflect the steps to be taken when an error is exposed and the costs per day for correcting these problems. Your contract also should state who is responsible for paying to correct these errors. More times than not, the simple method is to bill the owners and let them settle with the architect or designer.

Your contract also should state compensation due you for delays linked to plan errors and omissions. Figure out ahead of time what your overhead and operating expenses are on a daily basis for the project and then include a per-day penalty for delays.

Avoid problems

To minimize potential difficulties, your contract should define the:

- Architect's responsibilities

- Builder's responsibilities

- Owner's responsibilities

- Procedure for resolving plan problems discovered in the field

- Procedure for resolving errors, omissions, code compliance issues, site placement, and subdivision compliance.

Ultimately, you work for the owner. The owner has signed your contract. The architect and designer also are employed by and work for the owner. Just as your builder specifications take precedence over those of the architect's, so too should your determinations of responsibility and procedures for resolution.

Many architects have standard disclaimers placed on their plans that minimize their role should errors and omissions occur. A common disclaimer on the first page (usually the site plan) states: "All numerical dimensions are to be taken off of the plans. Scaling details on the plans for dimensions may not be accurate."

Such a disclaimer puts anyone scaling the plans in default. A disclaimer that disallows scaling of the plans causes further havoc in that custom doors and windows often must be ordered ahead of time before the rough openings are framed in.

> **Example**: The plans call for a 36-inch wide door at a specific opening, but when the framing begins there is not enough room for the 3-0 door and the 5-inch casing on each side. What procedures should be followed? Who compensates you for the time delay and possible change in materials?

During the actual construction of the home, a builder that discovers a conflict or problem with the plan or intended look sought by the architect or owner should note the problem as soon as possible with a change order. This alerts all parties to the situation and generates a written document that requires action on the intended solution.

Trying to solve the problem without bringing it to the attention of the architect or owner may lead to trust and accountability problems later. Know the line that separates builder and designer responsibilities. It will save you time, anguish, and money in the long term.

Omissions can be frustrating because custom projects often call for unique solutions. Sometimes errors, and altered, adjusted, or changed codes can throw a monkey wrench into the entire production schedule. Document the condition with a change order and outline a solution. Make sure the change order includes all details relating to the problem, including anticipated delays and additional costs. Case Study #9.2 provides an example of how a builder used contract language to put the responsibility for an omission on the architect.

Anticipate Common Field Problems

Common field problems that are typically encountered during custom home construction are noted by category below.

CASE STUDY #9.2

Stick to Your Responsibilities

A builder enters into a custom home project during the design stage. He works with and consults the owner and architect on issues such as time, materials used, and cost of the completed home. The footprint of the house is staggered and the two-dimensional elevations are sketchy regarding the full exterior picture of all areas of the house.

During the framing stage the architect and owner are inspecting the framing as part of a draw request. The owner notices two rooms on the north wing of the house that do not have high windows framed in. The architect indirectly inquires to the builder, "Oh I guess you're going to cut those window openings in later?" The builder responds: "No, there aren't any high, transom windows in either of those rooms."

Both owner and architect disagree with the contractor. The plans are reviewed and it is verified that the windows are not shown on the window schedule, any of the exterior elevations, or on the floor plan or framing plan.

The owner then makes the comment: "I assumed those windows were in those two rooms and I'm not funding the draw request until somebody puts them in. You two are responsible and the house is unbalanced without those windows."

Resolution: The builder stated that if the architect would buy the windows, the builder would install, trim, and finish the units. The architect refused and wanted to exchange future leniency on the builder's work as a tradeout.

The builder politely removed himself and visited his attorney to review the situation and the applicable language in the contract. The attorney recommended issuing a change order with a deadline date and the cost for performing the completed work.

The draw request remained open and unfunded. The deadline date came and went without a signed change order.

The builder again returned to his attorney and reviewed the situation. The attorney contacted the owner and reviewed the legal considerations and the position of the builder.

The owner approved the draw request, signed, and paid for the window change order and fired the architect. The change order costs were drawn against the final design fee payment to the architect.

Appliances. These products are modified annually for rough opening sizes, clearances, venting requirements, cabinet panel sizes, etc. Changes most often impact the cabinet layout design in kitchens and utility rooms and can cause problems with drawers, doors, pullouts, etc.

Base and casing. Make sure the trim details are spelled out in the specifications. Are some doors to be trimmed with ripped-down casing or the door hung several inches from the wall so full width casing can be installed?

The specifications impact the height of the exposed base at varied heights of floor coverings. Watch for door and window casing that might not align in both the vertical or horizontal planes, etc. Electrical boxes mounted adjacent to door jambs without consideration for wide, custom door casing also can lead to an unhappy owner and costly corrections.

Code compliance. Many building inspection departments emphasize and prioritize different elements that go into the home. Because codes constantly are being changed, adjusted, and adopted, it is more common than not to run into a compliance issue during construction. The plan-check submittal procedure eliminates some of these issues, but the field inspector has the final word.

Your contract should contain wording that protects you from changes and modification costs required by the city or municipality. Your contract should note what code book is being used to construct the project. Then, if a compliance issue arises from the latest addition of the Uniform Building Code (UBC), the contract states in black and white the set of rules you are following.

Municipalities, subdivisions, and design committees remove, alter, and add local ordinances to the building code. Examples of some of the exception problems in my building area include: woodstoves, outdoor jacuzzis (hot tubs), efficient water consumption appliances, limitations on exterior bar-b-ques, television dishes, exterior lighting restrictions and limitations, landscaping restrictions, and privacy requirements. Many of these conditions are subject to field interpretations.

Doors. Door sizes can be adjusted easily. The best method, however, is to order the doors with accurate information. Double check the door sizes (widths) between the door schedule and the door placements. Experience has demonstrated that the schedule and floor plan often have different door sizes. Find out which is correct. Changing the casing size after the plans are complete often changes the door sizes.

Entry doors. Most custom homes have a unique entry-door system design that is coupled with windows (operable or fixed), custom glazing, sidelights, an overhead transom, or a combination of these with other detailing such as stonework or millwork. Door hardware can be a problem for custom doors that are thicker than 1.75 inches. Making these elements work together can be difficult. The contractor has ultimate responsibility. Your task is to make it work.

Floor coverings. Due to the enormous variety of floor covering treatments, the prep work involved during construction is sometimes limited by the intended floor covering. Slabs are depressed or raised. Support framing is adjusted and modified per finish floor requirements and specifications. Certain detailing occurs to accommodate the abutment lines of wood floors to carpeting for an even transition, etc. Doors (inswing) with fixed thresholds are installed with the intent of functioning with a certain thickness of finished floor. Heights, depths, and transitions of floor coverings can be a potential problem area. Pay close attention. Most of these problems arise when changes are made in the floor covering selections as the home nears completion.

Subdivision code compliance. The accuracy of the plans, site layout, setback and height restrictions, etc., is the liability and responsibility of the architect and landowner. This includes any exterior feature, geometry, color, environmental impact, landscaping plan, or view disturbance of other properties adjacent or within close vicinity of the custom home project.

Make sure your contract states that you are following the plans and are not the compliance officer to the design review committee for the subdivision.

Windows. Windows come in nearly every conceivable shape, size, and dimension. Typical in custom home design, there is a stacked agglomeration of window units, combined for an overall design element. In certain circumstances, the windows might not align vertically or horizontally both inside and outside the home. This commonly occurs in fixed window units stacked over or adjacent to operable units.

My experience has been that these minor alignments do not become evident until the window package is delivered and assembled in the openings. Solutions vary from simple trim adjustments to a total reframing of the window opening. Work with a window brand you understand. It will minimize surprises.

10

Join the Team Early in the Process

Custom home projects are cumbersome, detailed, and expensive. The variety of products, textures, and finishes selected by both the architect and owner, when combined with unique design features, often make it difficult to prepare an accurate cost estimate and write specific, protective contract language.

Preparing a cost estimate that is well researched and documented is even more difficult given the time constraints associated with most projects. (Remember if you cannot do a proper estimate, for whatever reason, do not become involved with the project.)

Because custom homes are complicated projects and there are problems associated with proper and realistic cost estimates, a new business practice has been occurring more frequently in the marketplace.

Commonly called value engineering, the general contractor is hired by the owner and/or architect to review the plans and specifications as they are developed and to offer advice with regard to cost and complexity.

Builders are a valuable asset to the design, planning, and budget team. Your expertise and experience have value.

It is an ideal situation because the contractor is paid for his or her professional advice and expertise. Plus, the contractor is able to provide input to minimize the need for costly change orders and plan alterations.

When a project is value engineered the contractor and architect, along with subcontractors and suppliers, review the plans and specifications and then make adjustments and recommendations to bring the project's costs in line with the owner's budget.

I have employed value engineering in custom home projects on several occasions to the benefit of all parties involved.

In the long term, the synergy between the architect and builder achieved through value engineering provides the owner with a better home. The architect is less burdened with researching cost and labor information, and the builder gains knowledge from the architect with regard to new products, applications, and structural technology.

Too often the contractor is brought on as the caboose on the fast moving train, when in reality his or her expertise was needed months ago up in the locomotive to help plot the project's direction and momentum.

Another advantage to value engineering is that the builder and architect become comfortable working together as a team. Two heads are better than one. It is always better to develop an early working relationship between these two professionals, rather than jumping into maximum contact under the pressure of solving a design problem during the construction phase.

As a paid consultant, the contractor is suddenly elevated to the status of a true professional. The owner is paying for hard-earned advice, expertise, and knowledge. Historically, this has not been the case. Many, many custom home builders have been brought in to offer their knowledge on a custom project's open-ended details without being "hired on." All too often, builders are not paid for their time and efforts and subsequently are not selected to construct the home.

Implement Value Engineering

So you have heard the idea and the justifications for it, but how do you implement value engineering in your marketplace?

Work up a document or contract that spells out what you can offer and what you and your company will provide to the owner and architect during the design phase. In the contract, outline your fee, your responsibilities, and specifically what your company will provide. Figure 10-1 is a sample value engineering consulting agreement.

FIGURE 10.1 Preconstruction Value Engineering Consulting Agreement

Contractor:

Mr. Gerald R. Davenport
Davenport Contracting, Inc.
1234 W. Appalachian Way
Fresno, California 95528
(213) 555-1212

Owner:

Mr. John A. Smith
1515 North Main Street
Visalia, California 95528
(714) 555-1212

This agreement is made between the parties named above, Mr. John A. Smith (owner) and Mr. Gerald R. Davenport of Davenport Contracting, Inc. (consultant) to enter into a consulting arrangement with regard to the following construction project:

Smith Residence Custom Home
Lot 57 Sequoia Mountain Development
2557 E. Tall Pines Way
Fresno, California 95528

Owner is in the process of planning, designing, and budgeting a custom home project to be constructed on Lot 57, Sequoia Mountain Development. Owner agrees to hire the consultant (Davenport Contracting, Inc.) to provide the following work for the consideration of $10,000.00.

1. Work with Ron Abrams of RCA Architects on selection of materials, code compliance, and weekly review of design process.

2. Provide cost estimate information as needed by the architects during the design phase.

3. Coordinate survey, topography, and soils test (as needed). Services to be paid by the owner.

4. Provide and coordinate bid, cost estimate information for the owner within 30 days of the completion of the plans.

5. Owner has the sole option to proceed with the project and hire any general contractor. There is no obligation, written or implied, to the consultant.

6. Davenport Contracting, Inc. agrees to credit the amount rendered for their consulting services if awarded the contract to construct said residence. Consulting fee will be applied to the payment of Draw #1.

Owner	Date Consultant	Date

Use this contract for your consulting services during the design phase or as a tool that facilitates payment to you for the work you do. With this contract, you are not committed to building the project. Being involved early, however, provides you with compensation while giving you some breathing space to evaluate the circumstances involved. The contract gives you the ability to make a decision to proceed and build the project, or to politely back out due to timing, cost limitations, personality conflicts, etc.

Prepare an Agreement

Typically, the consulting agreement is one of two types.

Design/cost consulting. The contractor agrees to work with the architect and owner to review the design phase and offer advice, cost analysis, and practical information as the plans are generated. The fees can be structured on an hourly or fixed-fee basis. If the contractor does in fact build the project, the fees can be deducted from the final contract price, if desired. The owner pays for the advice of the contractor and in return receives the value of that expertise.

Cost estimate. When the plans are either nearing completion or completed, the contractor is brought in as a paid consultant to review the plans and specifications and generate a cost estimate. The contractor's risk is minimal because he or she is being paid for their time. The owners, in turn, can be assured that this is money well spent because they will obtain a thorough, professional estimate instead of one generated hastily. Preparing a cost breakdown or cost estimate on a fully detailed, 10,000-square-foot custom home, is not an overnight process.

In today's marketplace, fees range from $5,000 to $10,000 or they can be based on an hourly rate or percentage of the project cost. You also could discuss the fee schedule with the architect and be flexible so that the professional fees are in line with the architect's and owner's expectations. Don't chase away a potential client with excessive fees.

Your advantage as the builder is being able to rub elbows with the involved parties before committing to the project for an extended period of time. Requesting payment for professional services rendered will quickly separate quality, results-minded clients from people seeking free expertise. After all, does anyone ever get a free appraisal?

11

Anticipate Problems

Custom home builders have a difficult task. They must manage people and materials while coordinating with mother nature and chance, often for a period of 12 months or more. Add to these responsibilities the need to cope with the emotions of the owner and it's surprising that any contractor ever makes a profit.

Anticipate problems. Experience can help minimize problems, but a number of uncontrollable variables will always be present. Your ability to bend without breaking will help maintain your bottom line.

Don't let Murphy's Law* visit your project. Utilize your history and experience to assure smooth sailing on future custom home projects.

Take Preventive Measures

Anticipating problems is one of the contractor's main responsibilities. The ability to take preventive measures and solve problems before they occur is what separates profitable contractors from all others. These builders

*Murphy's Law is named after Edward A. Murphy, Jr., a U.S. engineer who formulated the saying in 1949.

know that it is more expensive to correct problems, than to resolve them before they occur.

The overall answer to minimizing problems is good management. Your profit percentage is directly proportional to your management performance. The steps to good management are based on experience, organization, and anticipation. Making a profit is only part of the battle. Retaining your hard-earned profit and not plowing back dollars into the project to correct mistakes is also a challenge.

"I know this is the 19th color sample, but . . ."

Assigning true blame and fault for mistakes is something that most builders have to train themselves to do. Being aware of the excuse phase and the ability to avoid past mistakes is part of the experience curve that leads a contractor to profitability.

The list of excuses is endless. Results are important. Stay focused on the project's quality and completion date. Learn from past mistakes so you don't repeat them again.

Manage Effectively

Effective management of a custom home project translates into a profit for the contractor. The formula is simple. Ask yourself some pertinent questions about the project, using the steps outlined below.

1. Is the project bid properly?

   - Make sure the plans and specifications are of good quality.

   - Is this a project your company can handle?

   - Are the time frame and budget within reason?

   - Secure written bids from all subcontractors and suppliers.

   - Calculate volumes, areas, and quantities; translate these into costs. Verify this information against subcontractors' and suppliers' bids. They can make mistakes, too!

- Fill out your bid form accurately and completely. Do not guess!

- If you do have to guess at a cost, guess high.

- Evaluate this project against previous jobs. Note difficult phases, potential weather problems, costs for specialty items, subtle expense items such as low productivity, downtime, freeze problems, protection of equipment and labor, vandalism, utility costs, etc.

2. Do the contract, allowances, draw schedules, and specifications meet your company's needs?

3. Can you realistically complete the construction schedule?

4. Are you set up to follow through on the paperwork: change orders to correct problems and letters to owners, such as progress reports, decisions needed, etc.

Legal problems are compounded by improper paperwork and documents that lack signatures. Don't avoid telling an owner bad news—it just delays the resolution. Be responsible and professional—inform the owner in a timely fashion. Avoided issues don't go away.

5. Is the job evaluation checklist complete?

- Did you receive firm cost quotes from subcontractors and suppliers? Are the prices, volumes, and costs based on accurate information?

- Have you anticipated the impact of weather changes, time allotments, and open-ended costs for all construction categories?

- Do you have the time to properly manage this job?

- Is this job within your experience range? Does it exceed it by 10 percent or 100 percent? Knowing when to say no is an attribute.

- What is your opinion on the caliber of the owners, the bank, the architect, and designer? Will they be working with you or against you?

- Does your bid amount and construction time meet the goals of the owners? If the person overseeing you has goals that are nearly impossible to meet, should you pursue the job or excuse your company?

■ Will your company be in control of this job or will it be con-
trolled by others—architect, bank, owner, subcontractors, or
suppliers? What can you do to minimize your exposure? Make
note of any anticipated problems in the specification category.
Address these subjects in written form to make problem resolution simpler, faster, and cleaner.

If you read through this checklist and find negative answers to several
questions, then consider avoiding the job. Starting a job with exposed
problems is an accident waiting to happen. Taking a job for the wrong
reasons could call up Murphy's Law and encourage whatever can go
wrong to go wrong. The project under consideration might drag down
some of your existing jobs and fill your time allotments so you cannot
take on better work.

The logic for making informed decisions is sometimes confused and
interwoven with the need to make money and generate income. Making
informed decisions should include only an evaluation of the positives and
negatives. Base your decision on these facts.

Ultimately, the goals of your company, the scope of work your company can handle, and the position of your company in the marketplace is
determined by your ability to be a good manager. Making informed decisions based on known facts is part of the profit equation.

Minimize the Impact of Construction Conditions

Some examples are noted here to minimize the impact of some construction circumstances. Noting these issues as footnotes in the specifications
will ease any potential misunderstandings.

Example 1: Stonework

The stone veneer selected for this project is available from a
quarry located out of state. The lead time specified for ordering the "Dendrite Speckled Flagstone" is 90 days. Because
the stone is a mined, natural material, color variations from
the approved sample may occur in the actual stone received.
The stone is a prepaid, custom order product that cannot be
restocked or returned.

Example 2: Hardware Doors

The hardware door allowance is $4,090. This allowance
amount includes the purchase, packing, shipping, and labor

to install costs for all door hardware for the Smith Residence. Because the hardware was not selected at the time the contract was being prepared, labor for installation will be invoiced at $42.50 per hour.

Contractor has advised owner that door hardware products are special order items that generally take 8 to 10 weeks for delivery. Contractor recommends that hardware be selected by owner no later than October 10 to avoid project completion problems.

Allowance Determination:

16 doors × $135 per lock	=	$2,160
Entry door × $500 per entry	=	500
16 doors × $10 per hinge × 3 hinges per door	=	480
Hardware labor estimate	=	800
Freight and shipping	=	150

Example 3: Floor Coverings

Carpet selected was Karastan 4527 "Arabian Winds" berber, 15-foot-wide roll material, installed over 3/16-inch Omalon pad #3489, density .345 pounds per yard.

Because carpet is a special order item that exceeds the industry standard 12-foot roll, the carpet is nonrefundable and may not be returned once the order is placed. Contractor will require a signed change order documenting permission by owner to order the carpet. Order lead time is 16 weeks. Contractor recommends that owner selections be confirmed no later than June 15th.

As part of the contract documents, builders should prepare and include an owner decision summary list. This document lists what decisions are needed and the due dates for those decisions. Figure 11.1 provides an example of an owner decision summary list.

FIGURE 11.1 Decision Summary List

Smith Residence
Forest Meadows Lot 59
4529 E. Aspen Grass Drive
Flagstaff, Arizona 86001

Subject	Lead Time	Selection	Date Decision Needed
Concrete Patio Color	1 week		January 5
Roof Tile Color	3 weeks		March 10
Door Hardware	10 weeks		April 12
Carpet	16 weeks		June 15
Shower Glass	3 weeks		July 31

All selections will be confirmed in writing before builder orders the materials. Special order items are nonreturnable or refundable.

12

Evaluate
Past Projects

Once you complete a project, it is helpful to evaluate the work and prepare a written summary for later reference. Ideally, the one-page evaluation sheet analyzes the project's profitability. The summary includes a description of problems and steps that can be taken to avoid these mistakes in the future.

Learning to evaluate your company's performance will help define your company's strengths and weaknesses. This knowledge in turn will enable you to target projects and quickly ascertain whether certain jobs fit within your company's scope of expertise.

When a project has good results and good profit, the reasons for that success can be a base evaluation point for future jobs. When the same things happen over and over, the written record lets you go back and review several similar job summary sheets to refresh your memory. The sheets remind you what worked well and what to avoid on the next project. Figure 12.1 is a sample project evaluation sheet.

Be your own best critic. Your past projects are a cornucopia of information waiting to be used to hone the profitability of future projects.

FIGURE 12.1 Project Evaluation Sheet

Project name: John and Mary Doe Residence

Project address: 1234 Sunset Vista Road, Roanoke, Virginia

Subdivision: Forest Meadows

House description: 4,820 sq. ft. (livable)

1,150 sq. ft. (garage)

Size: 5 bedrooms, 4 baths, ranch-type home on level lot; 5:12 hip roof system; large 130 ft. long driveway.

Gross job income: $567,994.40

Base contract: $538,640.00

Change orders: $29,354.37

Number of change orders: 12

Contract cost per sq.ft.: $117.84 ($567,994.40/4,820 sq. ft.)

• Builder cash cost per sq. ft.: $90.52 ($436,306.40/4,820 sq. ft.)

• Includes office overhead fees, superintendent labor costs, and insurance.

Builder net profit: $131,688.00

Builder percent profit: 30.18 percent = ($117.84 − $90.52/$90.52)

Construction period: 335 days (10 months)

Notes:

1. Plans were well detailed and clear as to work to be done.

2. Architect was easy to work with.

3. Building inspector called for seven special inspections at $80 per inspection. Cost was not bid into the project.

4. Driveway completion at end of job was tricky due to size of driveway and other trades accessing the job while driveway was being poured.

5. Scope of changes was small.

6. Bank was late on several draw inspections.

7. Utility trenching was underbid.

8. Made profit of $17,202.18 on 12 change orders.

Overall opinion: Good project.

If you rate the project you are evaluating poor or difficult, revisit the circumstances and take the time to critique why it was a difficult job. Ask yourself some key questions:

- Was the job out of your company's usual scope?

- What were the work and time requirements; were the details complicated, the plans poorly detailed?

- What phases of the job were problematic?

- What work forces were problematic—bad subcontractors, slow suppliers, materials delivered were broken or incorrect?

- Was your bid inaccurate? Where were the weak spots?

- Was the owner or architect meticulous and a perfectionist?

- Were the plans and specs poorly defined so your company got raked over the coals and the owners got more than they paid for?

Some additional questions to ask or consider about each project are suggested below. Working up your own list of reference information and questions will put you on the self-evaluation road faster.

- What was your return on energy, time, manpower, risk, and liability? Were you able to complete the paperwork? Was there adequate effort in the field on site management and quality? Was your bid accurate? Did you maximize your return on change orders?

- What worked well at the office? What office tasks need improvement?

- Where were most of the mistakes made?

- Which subcontractors and suppliers are performing well for your company? Which need improvement? Which subcontractors or suppliers should be replaced?

- Did the multiunit townhouse job that took 10 months to complete earn more income for your company than the custom home project that had the same gross sales dollars and took 14 months to complete?

- Viewing the big picture: What project would you do again?

- Which market contacts tend to yield the best projects and owners: real estate agents, word of mouth from past owners, advertising, membership in the home builders association, service club contacts, etc.?

Some of the conclusions you can draw are exemplified when you group questions and answers. When a future project presents itself, scan through the evaluation sheets and pull those jobs that closely resemble the proposed project. Use historical data to put the new project in perspective and decide whether you should bid the job.

Your company's past history might dictate that this type of job is not as profitable for your company as other types. Unless some piece of information has dramatically changed, you might be better off passing over the job and searching for another that is historically more profitable for you.

Analyze the Financial Data

When you complete the financial portion of the evaluation, make sure that you accurately record the costs and individual amounts. If you don't, or the numbers are jumbled or untraceable, then the information will not be helpful later.

Postponing financial analysis is akin to avoiding responsibility. Financial information and its analysis are the most important information that you can have at your fingertips.

Develop a Business Summary

Another type of helpful historical review is a business summary of the company's operations and projects for the past year. The document summarizes information you can use as an overall indicator of what direction your company should pursue in the coming year. Figure 12.2 is an example of a business summary.

Review the summarized information before you enter into your next project for invaluable insight. The summary information enables you to prioritize your workload and objectives on a path that will help you reach your overall goals.

FIGURE 12.2 Annual Business Summary

Company Conclusions: Smith Builders 1998 (10 Projects Completed)

1. Profits for homes 2,500 to 3,500 sq. ft.
   + Smaller homes 2,500 sq. ft. plus had quick completions.
   + Semi-custom homeowners are easier to deal with.
   − Subs were not as efficient in the larger customs.
   − Larger custom specialty items were hard to cost out and bid.
   + ABC Bank had best financing, draw pay performance.

2. Build on level lots in developed subdivisions
   − Houses on slopes had 28 percent higher cash costs.
   − Utilities hard to bid on houses on multiacre parcels.
   − Rock clause was not a moneymaker; it was breakeven.
   − Tree and resource protection was difficult and costly.

3. Value engineering (large customs)
   − Builder was not compensated for time and expertise.
   − Plan changes adds and deletes became very confusing.
   − Owners went back to original plan anyway.
   − Next time get retainer prior to any advice to architect or owner.

4. Design-and-build jobs are easier than owner and architect plans and specifications
   − Architect became one additional person to talk to.
   + ABC Architects easy to deal with.
   + Design-and-build plans had accurate cost estimates versus architect plans.
   − Architect plans had costlier detailing.

5. Location of jobs
   + Jobs in Shelby County were easier and more efficient.
   − Jobs with architect review committee had changes that were time consuming.
   − Stay away from jobs in Smithville.
   − 1-hour commute jobs had low productivity.

6. Allowances/change orders
   + Change orders had 72 percent profit margin on 3,000 sq. ft. homes.
   − Change orders had 16 percent profit margin on larger customs.
   − Allowances had 1 to 5 percent profit on medium and large customs.
   + Keep allowances to a minimum. Have owner select up front.
   − Updating subcontractors on change orders impacting them was confusing.
   − Owners on Lot 163 were always slow to sign and pay on change orders.

Sample Set
of Specifications

Addendum A: Specifications and Allowances

Smith Residence
1485 W. Johnson Road
Lot 57 Coconino Estates
Flagstaff, Arizona 86001
(602) 555-1291 (Home)

Specs reviewed, updated, and revised: _____(date)

Architect/designer: _____

Date of contract: _____

Date of plans: _____ , _____pages.

Building permit number: _____ City of Flagstaff

    Information contained in these specifications may be adjusted upon receiving the plans (approved plans) from the City of Flagstaff Building Department. Any changes will be communicated to the owners.

General Conditions

A. Owner to notify their homeowners insurance company of the project and notify contractor of any needed documentation or other requirements. Contractor requires homeowner to carry a course-of-construction insurance policy that can convert to a homeowners insurance policy at completion. This policy protects the landowner (owner of the project) from claims that cannot be levied against contractor, but can be levied against the landowner.

B. Soil conditions, property line setbacks, and zoning conditions are assumed to be correct. Contractor is constructing the project per directions of the owner. Contractor is not responsible for the condition of the lot, soil makeup, groundwater, radon conditions, or other inherent and native conditions of the owner's land.

C. Contractor will notify owner of any anticipated disruptions in utility services and an estimated length of time for the disruption.

D. Scrap articles generated during the construction project are the property of the contractor. Contractor will dispose of all scrap materials. Items deemed reasonable will be recycled. Owner keeping scrap materials must store them out of the way of construction activity.

E. Allowance Items: The cost of an allowance item is the cost paid by the contractor to the subcontractor or the retail cost of the material vendor that supplies the item. If the cash cost varies, plus or minus with the allowance amount, a credit or debit is issued including sales tax.

F. Labor for installation of allowance items will be billed at $45 per hour plus sales tax.

1. Appliances

Compactor: None

Cooktop: General Electric JGP 641 ES (4 burner, gas, white)

Cooktop vent: General Electric JXDV 66 (white)

Dishwasher: General Electric 1430 TWW (white)

Disposal: Insinkerator "Badger V" 1/2 HP unit

Microwave/convection oven: General Electric JET 344 (white) with trim kit

Oven: General Electric JKP 45 WP dual cleaning, wall ovens (white)

Refrigerator: Subzero 570 (48" wide, dual door freezer/refrigerator); panels (2) to match cabinetry.

Appliance warranty is limited to that of the manufacturer. Labor to replace faulty or defective units will be at an additional charge.

2. Cabinetry

Keystone Craftsmen Cabinet Company; as per plans.

Cabinet selection: Karman Cabinetry, American Craftsmen Series IV.

Cabinet box style: American 2-inch style face frame with exposed hinges (antique brass).

Door styles: Square raised panel (Door 500-RP) in kitchen, laundry, mudroom, bathrooms, family room, and entry bench; Recessed panel arch in master bath (Door 400 EA); Recessed panel square in kids' baths (Door 360 RP).

Wood species: Clear, red oak in all areas except white laminate with wood edge detail in laundry room.

Stain color: 571-B Medium Oak with (clear semi-gloss finish).

Hardware: $300.00 Allowance (50 knobs/pulls × $6.00). Installation is extra. Cabinet hardware must be selected by Sept. 20, 1998.

Appliance panels: Built-in refrigerator will require cabinet panels. Panels will be provided by Keystone Cabinet Co. and match surrounding kitchen cabinetry.

Cabinet Box Details: Vinyl wood grain interiors (standard).

Note: Cabinet layout plan will be drawn by the cabinet company and submitted to owner for review prior to finalization. Once approved by owner, order will be placed.

Owner viewed the cabinets, cabinet boxes, door styles, finishes, and sample installation of the units at the Keystone Showroom on August 13, 1998. All was approved and accepted.

3. Cleanup

Plastic garbage cans will be used to collect debris. A dumpster will be located onsite during some of the construction period due to its size and placement logistics. All construction debris, dirt, wrappings, boxes, packaging, and waste will be removed by the contractor.

Cleanup of the site will be done on a daily basis (light pickup) with a thorough cleanup occurring once per week. Any debris that can be picked up by wind, etc., will be discarded daily.

A portable construction toilet will be located at the site after footings are poured. Potty will remain until job is completed.

4. Closets

Shelving layout will be as per plans. Shelving and cleating material will be "closet-made" 4429 white wire materials in all bedroom closets, entry, and storage closets. Kitchen pantry will be 3/4-inch AB oak plywood shelving with 12-, 16-, and 18-inch depths per plans.

5. Concrete (Structural)

All concrete, grout, etc., is to be supplied by United Metro, Tanner Companies, Flagstaff Division. Tanner management to advise contractor as to pouring options due to changing weather conditions, etc. Contractor to make the final decision for long-term performance and maximum quality product finish.

Patio: See patio category.

Footing: 10-inch diameter × 24-inch width with two #4 parallel horizontal rebar. Vertical rebar on 48-inch centers except at earth retaining areas 24-inch on center.

Concrete will be minimum strength of 2,500 psi. Different strength material may be used depending on site conditions, weather, cure times, etc. Fibermesh concrete will be used in all washed ag concrete areas.

Sealer on any concrete is optional.

Accelerator may be used in concrete per the discretion of the concrete installation subcontractor.

Masonry cell grout will be 2,000 psi, minimum strength, at 28 days, 6 sack of cement per yard material.

6. Construction Access

Construction vehicles will park on the street and some will park in the temporary driveway and onsite. No parking will obstruct neighbors access to their driveways and care will be taken to minimize inconvenience to homes adjacent to the construction site. There may be some side or rear access to the property used during concrete pours and material deliveries for efficiency. All access areas will be restored to their pre-construction condition.

7. Countertops

Code and room name:

106 Guest bath counter:

- Ceramic tile.
- Arizona Tile 4x4 "Midnight Sun."
- C-Cure Grey 5701 grout (unsanded).

107 Bar counter:

- Laminate with a roll edge and 4-inch roll backsplash.
- WilsonArt 989-B "Summer Fawn."

108 Recreation room cab tops:

- Wood top to match cabinet finish.
- 1¥ oak edge on 3/4-inch oak plywood.

110 Dining room cabinet counter:

- Wood top to match cabinet finish.
- 1× oak edge on 3/4-inch oak plywood.

111 Kitchen counters:

- Tile (DAL white 4×4 as per tile specs).

111 Kitchen island:

- Tile (DAL white 4×4 as per tile specs).

111 Kitchen desk:

- Wood top to match cabinetry.
- 1× oak edge on 3/4-inch oak plywood.

115 Laundry/craft/utility room:

- Laminate tops with roll edge/splash.
- Formica 678 "Slate."

116 Powder bath:

- Synthetic marble top with formed elliptical sink.
- Arizona Marble Center 60-W "Winter White Swirl."

- Sink is elliptical 13-×-19-×-8-inch depth.
- Splash detail: rear and sides.
- Edge detail: 7/8-inch thick with 1/8-inch top roundover.

202 MBR bath counter:

- DAL 12×12 marble "Seafoam Green."
- Edge: 2-×-12-×-1/2-inch cut strips "Seafoam Green."
- Splash: 4-×-12-×-1/2-inch cut strips "Seafoam Green."

205 Kids' bath counter:

- Synthetic marble top and formed sink.
- Arizona Marble Center 48-V "Grey Swirl."
- Sink is Seashell sculpted: 13-×-19-×-8-inch depth.

207 Kids' bedroom window seat top: AB plywood with no finish. Owner to provide cushion.

208 Kids' bath counter: Same detail as bath #205.

8. Decking

N/A—none.

9. Driveway and Entry Sidewalk

All exterior concrete will be poured to a depth of 6 inches. Plans call out for 4 inches. Extra thickness will provide longevity due to harshness of climate and daily temperature fluctuations during the winter months.

Note: Using any ice melting chemicals, heating equipment, or rough abrasive snow removal equipment or methods will damage the long-term strength of the concrete finish and will void all warranty concepts and understandings regarding concrete appearance.

Driveway finish: Broom finish (no added color).

Entry sidewalk finish: Washed aggregate (no added color).

Stamped finish concrete (as per plans) was deleted 1-13-98 per owners. Layouts remain unchanged.

Entry sidewalk to angle from driveway edge to the front door. Layout to follow format of plan, but some adjustments may be made in the field due to site conditions, soil stability (to avoid a concrete support stemwall), and water runoff.

Sidewalk layout may be slightly adjusted to meander around existing trees. Tree positions as noted on plan are only approximate. Contractor will exercise care in preparing the form work and pouring concrete adjacent to plant life, but cannot guarantee their reaction to the ground disturbance or longevity.

Concrete will be formed and placed per plans. Material will be supplied by United Metro (Tanner Concrete) and of minimum strength 2,500 psi at 28 days.

Contractor may at its discretion use one or more of the following concrete reinforcement materials: nylon/fiberglass fibermesh, 610 welded wire mesh, or steel rebar for additional strength performance.

Pouring of the driveway concrete is planned on the construction schedule, but timing is at the discretion of contractor based upon weather, curing periods, access to the site, etc.

Heavy vehicle traffic is not allowed on the driveway for 10 days from when pour is completed.

10. Drywall

Standard 1/2-inch sheetrock in all locations as per plans. Type × 5/8-inch fire-rated sheetrock to be used on all garage surfaces (walls, ceilings). Green board sheetrock will be used in all "wet" wall areas. Code currently does not allow green board use in ceilings.

Corner bead: 3/4-inch round, galvanized.

Texture for house: Skip trowel.

Texture for garage: Skip trowel.

Window surrounds: Square bead on windows.

Drywall door surrounds: Square bead.

Note: Smooth wall finishes and wallpaper preparation are optional.

Walls may be paint-sealed prior to application of texture at the discretion of contractor.

11. Electrical Fixtures: $6,495 Allowance

Dining room fixture: $1,500

Recessed cans: (40) × $38 per can = $1,520

Exterior entry sconces: (6) × $125 per fixture = $750

Bulbs needed: $300

Ceiling fans: (5) × $250 per fan/blades/pole/rheostat = $1,250

Bedroom 3: $500 (for track lights).

Study ceiling fixture: $225

Exterior floodlights: (9) at $50 per fixture = $450

All fixtures are to be selected and purchased at the Light House, Flagstaff, Arizona, at retail prices. Prices noted above are the contractor's best estimate as to what the owner may spend on certain fixture selections. Bulbs and other necessary trim items will be charges against the overall value of the electrical fixture allowance. Contractor will not install or warrant owner provided fixtures.

Items charged to allowance include all electrical fixture items—recessed cans, recessed can trim, bulbs, interior and exterior fixtures.

Wiring, switches, plugs, bath fans, breaker box are not part of this allowance item.

Recessed cans: Juno IC 22 (6-inch diameter up to 75 watts of light).

Recessed can trims: Vaulted and soffitted ceilings—Juno Eyeball #229 (white); flat ceilings—Juno Black Baffle #24 (black).

Plugs, switches, and cover plates: Leviton brand, standard toggle style, ivory color, standard style switches, and plugs. Other colors are optional.

12. Electrical Wiring

200-amp electrical service is included with a single-service electrical panel. Location of the electrical subpanel is per plan. If electrical utility demands relocation of electrical breaker box for meter reading purposes, a change order will be issued.

The electrical service includes wiring for all plugs, switches, electrical appliances, fixtures, TV cable, telephone wiring, etc., placed in locations according to the plans. Installation of all trim, fixtures, etc., is included in this category.

Wiring is *not* included for possible under-cabinet lights in kitchen. Owner must decide on the under-cabinet lights by October 15, 1998. Change order will document selection and expense. Fixtures are charged against the electrical fixture allowance.

13. Excavation

All excavation is included for the driveway, footings, floor areas, patios in the footprint area of the plans. Rock removal (if required) will be at an additional charge. Dirt and rubble excavation is included with the contract. Loading, hauling, and dumping of rock, rubble, and dirt off the site is not included in the contract price.

14. Finish Materials

Front doors: Two 2680 × 2.0-inch thick at perimeter styles, multi-raised panel (24 panels of varying size), mahogany doors. Supplied by IWP, San Diego, California. Door opening width is 5 feet by 8 feet high.

Interior doors: Birch slab (solid core) 8-0 tall doors, per plan.

Garage to house door: Birch, flat panel, 1.75-inch solid-core fire door. Doors supplied by Kimmbal Door Co.

Baseboard: 3.25-inch pine (clear), colonial pattern (main level).

Casing (trim around doors and windows): 2.25-inch pine colonial.

Crown molding #374 profile (4-inch pine): Living and dining rooms at intersection of walls and ceilings.

Special details: None.

Note: The baseboard and casing noted are a basic cost item. Any additional selections or changes will be at an additional cost.

Wood ceilings: Family room, kitchen, breakfast nook, sunroom, and ceiling above hallway overlook into those areas. 1×6 T&G #2 STK pine, rough side out. Wood will be installed perpendicular to the roof rafters, which is also perpendicular to the outside walls. In all rooms, the wood joints will run "long ways" with the room size.

15. Fireplaces

Family room/recreation room dual-side fireplace: Marco ST42 dual-sided unit with polished brass frame, glass doors. Contractor/owner may select another brand of similar quality based on owner details and finish coordination.

Fireplace mantles: As per soffit/bookcase plan details.

16. Floor Coverings: $18,685 Allowance

Carpet selection:

Tile selection (floor only): _____

Vinyl floor selection: _____

Carpeted areas: Living, family, recreation room, all bedrooms, guest room, Dan's office, upper hallway, both sets of stairs.

Tile flooring: Kitchen, breakfast nook, sunroom, laundry, powder room, bar, kids' bath 1, kids' bath 2.

Vinyl flooring: Mudroom.

Wood flooring: None.

Carpet Selection:

- 1. 4,310 sq. ft. × 6 percent waste = 4,569 sq. ft.
- 2. 4,569 sq. ft./9 sq. ft. per sq. yard = 508 sq. yards
- 3. 508 sq. yards x $30 per yard = $15,240

Carpet to be supplied and ordered from Bing Bros. Carpet Co. Prices quoted are based on floor covering use per plans. Carpet waste, pad, installation labor may change based upon actual carpet selection.

Allowance calculation is assuming a plush carpet over 9/16-inch rebond pad (standard).

Prices will be quoted to owner. Order will be verified with a signed change order.

Carpet based on: Mohawk "Melody River" 17 colors, 12-foot rolls.

Tile selection: 1. 355 sq. ft. × 10 percent waste = 391 sq. ft. tile
2. 400 sq. ft. (tile ordered in 10 sq. ft. boxes).
3. 400 sq. ft. × $8 per sq. ft. (tile only) = $3,200
4. Labor charge is included for standard floor tile.
5. Grout cost using standard C-Cure colors included.

Vinyl selection: 1. 110 sq. ft. × 9 sq. ft. per sq. yard = 12.22 sq. yards.
2. 12.2 yards × $20 per sq. yard = $245
3. Vinyl roll width and pattern/layout could impact the vinyl needed for a specific room.

17. Garage Doors

Raynor brand, rough sawn, wood textured masonite exterior, 4-panel doors. Three doors sized at: 9 feet wide × 8 feet; Genie 1/2 hp opener are included for the doors. Doors are solid masonite. Insulated doors are optional. Doors require service check once per year to remain in good working order.

18. Glass

Bath glass: Standard 1/4-inch thick silver glass mirrors. Mirrors are width of vanity and standard finished height of 36 inches. Application is by mirror mastic adhesive and J mold above back splash.

MBR shower has a glass door and frame in rain drop glass/brass trim and frame. Guest bath: Rain drop/brass. Kids' bath shower: Rain drop/chrome.

Delete mirror for powder bath due to owner placing an oval mirror above sink vanity (per Mrs. John Smith, owner).

19. Hardware

Kwikset Titan "Cortez," polished brass (all doors).

Front entry: Kwikset "Pilgrim" by Copa, polished brass.

Deadbolts: Kwikset Titan single-cylinder units.

Note: Matching deadbolts (single-cylinder) are at exterior doors.

20. Heating (HVAC) System

Furnaces (2): 110,000 and 140,000 BTU, Trane, natural gas, forced air furnaces. Furnace filter system will be standard with hinged grills and fiberglass 3/4-inch thick filters. Electronic air cleaning devices are optional.

Thermostats: Honeywell T-87 (rotary dial thermostat).

Venting: Per code and manufacturer's specifications. Dryer vent to exhaust in soffit, exterior wall, or through the attic.

Air conditioning is *not* provided.

21. Insulation

Ceilings: R-38 (blown and batt fiberglass insulation).

Space limited ceiling areas: R-19, R-22, R-30.

Upper floors: R-22 fiberglass batt.

Exterior walls: R-22 fiberglass batt.

Interior walls: R-11 fiberglass batt.

Blown fiberglass insulation will be applied to any ceiling area where there is attic access.

Maximum insulation will be applied to all open void areas in the home. Insulation will be placed in virtually all nooks, crannies and spaces. R-22 exterior wall insulation is an upgrade from the standard code-required R-19 batt system.

22. Landscaping

All construction debris, material cuts, block chips, etc., will be removed and the terrain restored to a yard area similar to the condition found prior to construction. No landscaping materials are included. Also optional: landscape berming, tree removal, tree trimming, and tree wells.

Perimeter of the residence will be bermed and backfilled with a slope contoured away from the house of approximately 2 to 5 degrees. Backfill material will be the soil excavated from the footings.

Mulch, topsoil, cinders, cindersand, dirty cinders, etc., (fill dirt) is not included as backfill and site coverage material.

Finish landscaping is by others.

23. Lumber and Materials

Headers: #2 D-Fir (either solid wood or built-up beams depending on location to exposed rafter beams and the perimeter beam).

Wall studs—Exterior: 2×6 #2 Hem Fir, #2 Pine.

Wall sheathing: 15/32-inch OSB (oriented strand board).

Roof sheathing: 15/32-inch and 19/32-inch OSB, 4x8 sheets.

Soffit material: Rough sawn, 6-patch 3/8" T-111 plywood.

Rafters (exposed): Per plans.

Interior beams and rafters: Per plans.

Siding: 1×8, Cedar #2 STK (select tight knot)

Lap siding: See siding category.

Fascia: 2×10 and 2×12 #2 STK S1S2E (rough sawn) Spruce.

Roof pitch is a 4/12. Trusses will be used in all areas of roof framing where practical. Other areas will be "stick-framed" with D-Fir rafters or TJI "I" beam-type rafters depending on application. Truss company engineers are designing the roof framing plan and will submit to City of Flagstaff per approval.

- STK = select tight knot lumber grade.

- OSB = oriented strand board.

24. Masonry

As per plans with the following notes:

- Elevation of home is such that driveway at garage entry will slope to the street. Garage floor elevation above street level will be determined onsite per site conditions at the discretion of the contractor. Actual finished height will be 6 to 16 inches above the street level at the center of the street.

- Cement stucco (sand plaster finish/texture) is to be used on the masonry exposed stemwall areas.

- Grout color: Grey (standard mortar)

- #4 Rebar verticals at 48 inches on center in CMU block stemwall.

- 8x8x16 CMU ("grey" cinder block) as the standard masonry block, solid grouted with pea gravel grout, 2,000 psi minimum strength.

- Bond beam as per code.

- Masonry block will be finished to a sand plaster finish texture and pattern.

25. Painting and Staining

Materials will be supplied by Kelley-Moore Paints, Flagstaff, Arizona. Exterior is to receive paint or stain, 1 color, 2 coats. The first coat is a heavy "soaking" coat, followed by a second cover "misting balance" coat. Both coats are applied on the same day.

- Fascia is to receive an accent color, solid body paint.

- Additional exterior trim colors or accent colors are optional.

- Garage exterior surfaces to receive paint (no stain).

- Interior baseboard and casing are stained and lacquered.

- Interior sheetrock surfaces are painted, 1 primer color, 1 finish color, flat finish. Color: off white (Dix-Mix).

- Accent color at kitchen: _____. (Dark colors such as navy, forest green, magenta may be at extra cost due to coats, prep time, etc. Dark colors are also difficult to touch up.)

- Interior doors are stained and lacquered. (One-coat sealer, one-coat stain, 2 coats semi-gloss lacquer.)

- Interior wood ceilings are spray stained.

- Wiping stains for T&G wood ceilings will be an additional charge.

- Lacquering beams, wood ceilings, etc., will be an additional charge.

26. Patios (3)

Family room patio as per layout in plans, but extends out 10 feet further on each end with an eyebrow bend to connect the two sides. Square footage allowance: 760 sq. ft.; washed aggregate finish.

Covered patio area on the south side of garage is broom finish. No concrete color in either pour.

Guest room patio was deleted 6-29-98.

27. Plumbing

Kitchen sink: Kohler K-5941 "Brookfield" (white).

Kitchen sink faucet: Delta 21460 pull-out/stream/spray (chrome).

Disposal: Insinkerator 1/2 HP "Badger 5" (See appliance category).

Soap dispenser: Delta. Match faucet finish (chrome).

MBR sinks: Kohler K-2195, Pennington elliptical (china) sinks with 8-inch center set (white).

MBR sink faucets: Delta 3577 PB/RP 19530 PB (porcelain cross handles).

MBR toilet: K-3421 Wellworth Lite (PB handle) elongated bowl.

MBR shower valves (2): Delta 1448 PBLHP/RP19628PB (shower valve).

MBR tub model: Kohler "Victorian" K-770 white, cast iron.

MBR tub valve: Delta 2770PB/RP porcelain cross handles.

Guest bath sinks (2): K-2195 Pennington elliptical 4-inch (china) sinks.

Guest bath sink faucets: Delta 3567 with RP14788 PB.

Guest bath toilet: K-3421 Wellworth Lite (white).

Guest bath tub: None.

Guest bath shower valve: Delta 4546 "Scald Guard" (chrome).

Powder bath sink: K-2195 Pennington (white).

Powder bath sink valve: Delta 520 WFMPU (polished brass).

Powder bath toilet: K-3421 Wellworth Lite (white)/polished brass.

Kids' bath 1 sinks: Syn marble one-piece, oval, (white).

Kids' bath 1 faucets: Delta 520 WFMPU (chrome).

Kids bath 1 toilet: K-3421 Wellworth Lite (white)/chrome.

Kids' bath 1 tub: Kohler K-715 Villager (white) cast iron 5-foot tub.

Kids' bath 1 tub/shower valve: Delta 641 CP (chrome).

Kids' bath 2 sink: Syn marble one-piece, oval, white/chrome.

Kids' bath 2 faucet: Delta 520 WFMPU (chrome).

Kids' bath 2 toilet: K-3421 Wellworth Lite (white)/chrome.

Kids' bath 2 tub: Kohler K-715 Villager (white) cast iron 5-foot tub.

Kids' bath 2 tub valve: Delta 641 CP (chrome).

Laundry room sink: Kohler 170 laundry sink, cast iron (white).

Laundry room faucet: Delta 100 WF (chrome).

Bar sink: Elkay 174-C 13x13 stainless (3-hole).

Bar faucet: Delta 2172 SHP/RP15069.

Interior plumbing lines: Copper (Type L) water pipe; ABS drain, waste and vent (no PVC).

Hose bibb locations: Per plans. Plumbing contractor may want to relocate hose bibbs due to freeze protection considerations.

Water heaters: A.O. Smith or Bradford White (Champion) brand 50- and 75-gallon natural gas water heaters. Heaters have a built-in insulation system. Water heater exterior wrap blankets are optional.

Gas BBQ hookup at patio: Owner to indicate location.

Hot water recirculation system: Lang pump will service the kitchen and kids' bathrooms. MBR bath, bar, guest bath are close enough to the water heater to not require hot water recirculation.

28. Porte Couchere

Per plans; area at driveway, ceiling to be flat, covered with T-111 rough sawn, no groove plywood siding. 1×2 Pine (rough sawn) Lath strips to be applied on 16-inch centers, the width of the ceiling, to trim out and enhance the appearance of the ceiling.

Ceiling over walkway to front entry: Same as above.

Framing system to be the same as that for the residence.

Roofing materials to be the same as that for the main residence.

Porte couchere will not be insulated.

29. Rain Gutters: $4,620 Allowance

Cost for gutter allowance is included in contract price. Heat tapes are optional (500 linear feet × $4.20 per linear foot installed = $4620). Subcontractor is Northern Arizona Guttering Co.

30. Roofing

Roofing: Elk Brand, P-1, 30-year limited warranty, architectural shingles, "Weathered Wood" color.

Felt underlayment: Standard 15 lb. and 30 lb. felt.

Eaves and valleys: 90 lb. felt underlayment.

Flashing: Galvanized, 28-gauge metal.
    Roofing should be inspected twice yearly for its overall condition: loose or broken shingles, removal of pine needles, weather and ice damage, etc.

31. Sample Preparation

If owner requests contractor to prepare samples of color, drywall texture, wood stain, etc., there will be an additional charge of $75 per sample. This covers the time and effort in preparing such samples.

32. Security System

Prewiring costs are included for main doorways and motion detectors for thruway areas. Trim allowance for system is $2,200. Prewiring allows owners more choices in trimming the system at home completion or at a later date. Subcontractor is Aegis Security Systems Co.

33. Sidewalks (See driveway and patio categories)

Porte couchere sidewalk is 6 feet in width and washed aggregate finish. No added color. Aggregate is 3/4-inch and smaller pit stone. Owner saw and approved sample finish per the driveway at the Smith Residence, Flagstaff, Arizona, on 1-19-98.

Rear side patio and walk are broom finish, no color.

Stamped finish concrete was deleted by owners 1-13-98.

34. Siding (Exterior)

Siding: 1×8 Cedar #2, STK, rough sawn, bevel lap siding.

Soffits: 3/8-inch T-111, rough sawn plywood, 6-patch, (no groove).

Fascia: 2×10 and 2×12 rough sawn S1S2E Spruce, #2 STK.

Window and door trim: 1×4 S1S2E Spruce #2 with a square edge.

35. Skylights

Per plans; Velux brand; clear glass with bronze aluminum frames.

36. Specialty Items

Entertainment package/stereo system/speakers: Not selected or identified at time of contract preparation. Selections are to be completed by owner on or before July 10, 1998. Subcontractor is Stereo System Specialists, Sedona, Arizona. Equipment, details, installation locations, and cost will be noted with a change order. Contractor's estimate for such a system for this project is $25,000 plus sales tax.

Intercom: N/A

Gas BBQ: Fire King 123 XZ, 48-inch-width model in stainless steel. Unit located in masonry BBQ structure per plans. Height of grill is 42 inches above finished grade directly in front of the BBQ.

Mailbox: To be located at the southeast intersection of driveway and street. Masonry column is 24 inches square by 56 inches tall. Metal USPS approved mailbox to be installed at 42 inches above street grade. Mail person will approve location. Column will be veneered with stone to match the house.

Spa: Was deleted from plans 2-13-98 by owners.

Sprinkler tap/hookups: Plumbing contractor will provide a 1-inch copper line (Type M) at the utility stub and mount area on the west side of the garage. Sprinkler system and landscaping by others after home has been completed.

Telephone jacks: Per plans with a 10-pair wire to all locations.

TV antenna/satellite/DSS: N/A (See Entertainment System above).

Water, gas, TV, telephone and electrical lines or tap points for future sprinkler systems, spa locations, yard lights, etc., are not included in the plans. Owners to notify contractor of any special requirements concerning these items prior to commencement of construction.

Window coverings/treatments: By others.

37. Stonework

Dunbar Stone Co., Kingman, Arizona.

Stone: Tawny Beige flagstone, set on edge.

Size: Varies 2 to 10 inches thick and larger.

Grout: Standard grey mortar.

Joints: 3/4 to 1 inch.

Owner should be aware that samples of stonework are approximate. Stone is mined and will vary slightly in color and texture. Stonework is modeled after the stone veneer at Desert Vista Country Club.

38. Tilework

Floor tile is not included. All tilework costs are included in contract and will be Dal Tile products #4100, in various colors selected, semi-gloss 4.25-×-4.25-inch tile, installed over "Durock" with C-Cure brand ceramic tile mastic; grouted with 0-100 Glacier White, unsanded C-Cure grout. Backsplash to be surface bullnose 4.25-×-4.25-inch single tile with edges, double bullnose.

Layout pattern: Square with standard 1/8-inch grout joints.

Also see countertops and floor coverings categories.

39. Tree Removal and Site Preparation

Tree trimming, thinning and removal once the initial site prep is completed will be at an additional charge.

Protection of terrain, rocks, and trees: Contractor will provide access to the jobsite with one main path. Trees adjacent to the direct construction vehicle access will be shielded with carpet pad, plywood, etc., to facilitate their protection from damages, scarring, etc.

Contractor will minimize disruption of utilities (gas and electric) due to relocations and taps. Utilities may be off during working hours, but every effort will be to restore operation by day's end.

40. Wallpaper

None specified. Wallpaper wall prep is optional.

41. Windows

Bronze, tan color, aluminum framed, dual glazed, high altitude windows. See the plan schedule for actual window sizes and other details. Window layout follows the revised plan.

Tempered glazing to be used adjacent to doorways, window seats, bath areas, etc., as per requirements by the Uniform Building Code (UBC).

Brand: Eagle; low-E coated, dual-glazed, insulated, awning, casement, double-hung, and fixed-style windows.

No UV protection is included. No shading film is included. Installation of such films will void warranty due to temperature variations. Dual-glazed window panels are warranted from fogging for a period of 5 years from the date of home completion.

Replacement labor for glass units will be at an additional cost. Interior and exterior work related to replacing glazing also will be at an additional cost.

Contractor	Homeowner	Homeowner
Date	Date	Date

B

Sample 10-Draw Schedule

Smith Residence
Lot 7 Rolling Hills Estates
Irving, Texas 77092

Contract Price: $595,000.00

The following schedule lists the percentage and amount of each draw along with the work that must be completed before the draw is paid.

Draw 1: 10 percent ($59,500) of contract price less the downpayment of $15,000 equals a net draw of $44,500.

- Building permit obtained
- Tree removal staking
- Tree removal
- Tree disposal
- Footing survey placement
- Footings dug and poured
- Masonry block stemwall built and grouted

- Utility trenching and equipment (grinder pump, propane tank) installed
- Exterior grading
- Backfill completed

Draw 2: 10 percent ($59,500) of the contract price

- Electrical service activated
- Floor framing completed
- Window package ordered
- Garage concrete floor poured and finished

Draw 3: 15 percent ($89,250) of contract price

- Wall framing completed
- Stonework prep completed
- Masonry fireplace completed
- Roof framing in-progress
- Exterior grading 90 percent completed

Draw 4: 10 percent ($59,500) of contract price

- Roof framing completed
- Stonework begun (10 percent completed)
- Rolled roofing underlayment (90 lb.) completed
- Metal roof flashing completed
- Skylight installation completed
- Roof tile order placed

Draw 5: 10 percent ($59,500) of the contract price

- Plumbing trim package ordered
- Plumbing rough-in completed
- HVAC (heating) rough-in completed

- Windows, exterior doors installed
- Window trim and siding in-progress
- Stonework 50 percent completed
- Patio pavers installed
- Framing punch completed; frame checked again

Draw 6: 10 percent ($59,500) of the contract price

- Exterior concrete work completed
- Electrical rough-in completed
- Electrical fixtures and trim ordered
- Alarm system wiring completed
- Insulation completed
- Cabinetry ordered
- Finishwork package ordered
- Garage doors ordered

Draw 7: 10 percent ($59,500) of the contract price

- Stonework 75 percent complete
- Siding completed
- Exterior woodwork stained, sealed, and finished
- Drywall hung, beaded, and taped
- Primer paint coat on drywall
- Drywall textured
- Finish coat wall paint applied
- Garage door installed

Draw 8: 10 percent ($59,500) of the contract price

- Furnaces installed and operating
- Finishwork in-progress (doors, window jambs, casing)

- Tongue-and-groove wood ceilings completed
- Stonework completed
- Appliances ordered
- Paint and stain in-progress
- Tilework rough-in in-progress
- Hardware order placed

Draw 9: 10 percent ($59,500) of the contract price

- Tilework completed
- Flooring rough-in and prep completed
- Electrical switches and plugs installed
- Roofing tiles completed
- Hardware order unpacked and checked

Draw 10: 5 percent ($29,750) of the contract price

- Electrical fixtures and plumbing trim, details completed
- Appliances installed
- Flooring completed
- Door hardware installed
- Final cleaning completed

*Note: Owner may withhold $2,500 until walkthrough and punch list is completed. Draw 10 is due and fundable upon passing final inspection.

Contractor Homeowner Homeowner

Date Date Date

Check out these "Basics"
from Home Builder Press...

Basic Business Management: *A Guide for Small-Volume Builders*
By Dorn Fowler

Increase your profits by refining your business management practices. **Basic Business Management** helps you set up the policies and procedures you need to become a more effective manager, run a more professional building business, and increase your margins. Each aspect of a complete management system is addressed:

- Management Activities
- Strategic Planning
- Marketing and Sales
- Legal Documents and Regulations
- Estimating and Scheduling
- Human Resources
- Accounting
- Financing
- Customer Service and Warranties

Basic Business Management answers the "whys" and "hows" of developing and implementing systems that will enable you to increase the productivity and efficiency of your resources.

Basic Construction Management: *The Superintendent's Job*
By Leon Rogers

No one person has more control over your building operations than the superintendent. **Basic Construction Management** provides information that will sharpen a superintendent's skills in maintaining budgets, preparing and meeting schedules, and ensuring quality control. Noted speaker and professor Leon Rogers places special focus on developing and managing systems to address key areas superintendents need to master:

- Project start-up
- Quality control and inspections
- Cost control
- Scheduling
- Construction team building
- Trade contractor management
- Working with the homeowner
- Safety management

Basic Construction Management also emphasizes how to computerize your scheduling and reporting systems. New managers can use this essential reference as a comprehensive training tool, while more experienced superintendents can brush up on the latest techniques and technologies.

To place an order or for more information, contact:

A Service of

Home Builder Bookstore®
National Association of Home Builders
1201 15th Street, NW
Washington, DC 20005-2800
(800) 223-2665
www.BuilderBooks.com